~ *Wrinkly Tin* ~

~ *Wrinkly Tin* ~

THE STORY OF CORRUGATED IRON IN NEW ZEALAND

Stuart Thomson

Stuart Thomson

STEELE ROBERTS
AOTEAROA NEW ZEALAND

'Wild Iron' (page 115) is reproduced courtesy of the estate of Allen Curnow. 'Rain on the roof' on page 121 (originally published in 1967 by George Braziller in *The Pocket Mirror*, currently available in *Poems and Stories*, Vintage 2004) is reproduced courtesy of the Janet Frame Literary Trust.

Colorsteel® prepainted steel and Zincalume®, a zinc/aluminium alloy coated steel product, are manufactured and marketed by New Zealand Steel. ColorCote® ZR8™, ZRX™, AR8™ and ARX™ are registered trademarks of Fletcher Steel Ltd, a Fletcher Building Ltd business.

National Library of New Zealand Cataloguing-in-Publication Data
    Thomson, Stuart, 1929-
    Wrinkly tin : the story of corrugated iron in New Zealand / Stuart Thomson.
    Includes index.
    ISBN 1-877338-70-2
    1. Sheet-metal, Corrugated—New Zealand—History. 2. Roofing,
    Iron and steel—New Zealand—History. I. Title.
    721.04471—dc 22

Cover design: Lynn Peck, Central Media Ltd

Photos: The kiwi on the cover and title page is a corrugated iron sculpture by Jeff Thomson. The page 1 photo of the musterers' hut on Shirlmar Station, near the Dunstan Saddle, is by Gilbert van Reenen, Clean Green Images (www.cleangreen.co.nz).
    Photos are credited where known, or are from the author's collection. All efforts have been made to identify photo sources; please contact the publisher with any additional information and we will amend future printings and note changes on our website.

STEELE ROBERTS LTD
Box 9321, Wellington, Aotearoa New Zealand
(04) 499 0044 • info@steeleroberts.co.nz • www.steeleroberts.co.nz

Contents

Late spring snowfall at Blue Range Hut, Tararua Forest Park.
SHAUN BARNETT/BLACK ROBIN PHOTOGRAPHY

Self-evident pride of man and friend
outside their hut in Northland,
circa 1910.

My house of tin that I live in
I think is really great
But I know I would be lonely
Without my dog called 'Mate'.

Foreword

I have long known Stuart Thomson as an expert on coated steel sheet and a skilled writer of erudite reports, so I am not surprised that from his lifelong love of corrugated iron this fascinating story has evolved. I was not expecting, however, to find that he is also a competent poet in the Jim Hopkins mould.

Stuart's book describes the role and the romance of corrugated iron in New Zealand and the debt the pioneers and their successors owe to this versatile, utilitarian material.

There are other reasons for the nation to be appreciative. The usage of galvanised sheet in New Zealand, probably the highest per capita in the world (about 64,000 tonnes total) was high enough in 1963, including some anticipated export business, to justify the installation of a modern continuous galvanising plant at Glenbrook as part of the establishment of our indigenous iron and steel industry.

A metal coating line (galvanising plant) with a nominal capacity of 100,000 tonnes per annum was commissioned in 1968. It operated on imported Japanese 'mother coils' of semi-finished cold rolled steel sheet and produced small galvanised coils, strip, sheet and corrugated iron for domestic and export markets. The positive cashflow from this operation was crucial in keeping the company afloat during nearly three years of problems while the iron and steel plants were extensively modified and commissioned.

In turn, following the optimisation of the iron and steelmaking process in the pilot plant at Glenbrook around 1980, markets for metal and prepainted steel sheet products, together with pipe and hot and cold rolled sheet and plate, justified building new iron and steel plants and installing hot and cold rolling mills and associated facilities. These were commissioned between 1982 and 1988.

At Glenbrook there is now a highly efficient and internationally competitive steelworks with a unique process, making 600,000 tonnes of products a year from Waikato coal and ironsand. New Zealand Steel Ltd is owned by BlueScope Steel Ltd of Australia and contributes, directly and indirectly, more than $2 billion annually to the New Zealand economy. Without the high domestic demand for corrugated iron over 40 years ago, all this may not have happened.

Sir John Ingram

I agree with Stuart that there is no point in trying to correct the term 'corrugated iron'. I even tend to use it myself, if only to avoid correcting the uninitiated and answering questions on the difference between iron and steel!

Thanks, Stuart, for a very good read.

Sir John Ingram CBE, Dist. FIPENZ, Dist. FIDNZ
Chief Executive, New Zealand Steel Ltd, 1969–87

New Zealand Steel's mill, looking south towards Waiuku. Steelmaking in the foreground.
NEW ZEALAND STEEL

Introduction

This is the story of corrugated iron ~ a part of our history that has touched every one of us. A few people hate it, but more of us like it or even love it.

Returning Kiwis recognise home by the corrugated iron roofs perched on hilltop houses. New Zealand is inconceivable without the stuff.

What to call it is a problem. Corrugated iron has been called many things: wrinkly or wriggly tin, roofing tin, symmetrical sinusoidal, CI, GCI (galvanised corrugated iron), corru, galvo, 'the galvanise', ripple and furrowed iron. Recently the adjective 'corrugated' has become a noun, and corrugated iron is now often called *corrugate*.

In the only other New Zealand book on the topic, the 1983 *Corrugated Iron in New Zealand*, co-editor (with David Mitchell, John Maynard & Warren Viscoe) Geoff Chapple describes its "unremitting ripple" in the background of so many iconic images of New Zealand.

Actually, corrugated iron is neither iron nor tin. Technically it's corrugated steel, but has been widely known as corrugated iron or 'tin' for decades. Any attempt to correct the term would fail, so generally in this book we'll call the material *corrugated iron*.

The first corrugated iron came out on the boat with the early British settlers. Soon a regular demand was met by the small ships that sailed to the new colonies in Australia and New Zealand.

This is the story of 'wrinkly tin', and how the familiar black sand on our beaches eventually became the corrugated iron on your roof.

The pictures and verse are meant to offset the prose. Like the material itself, they are unpretentious and unassuming. The limerick is said to be the lowest form of wit and the author makes no claim to the title of poet ~ after reading this book you probably will agree. Raising a slight inward smile is sufficient reward. With apologies to Rudyard Kipling:

> Gold for the mistress, silver for the maid
> Copper for the craftsman, cunning at his trade.
> "Good!" said the Baron, sitting in his hall,
> "But corrugated iron is master of them all."

JEFF THOMSON/PATAKA

New Zealand is a blessed land
Including heaps of iron sand
Herein iron's saga, frankly stated
Just how it's made and corrugated

The tactile nature of the material has its own attraction and does not deter would-be signwriters. It doesn't worry them that the wall ain't flat.
COLIN MARTIN

Tree huts: Above, on Waiheke Island.
COLIN MARTIN
Left: In the Coromandel.
PAUL THOMPSON, ALEXANDER TURNBULL LIBRARY PA12 1354 18

I had a little tree house
Nothing could be better
I shared it with a little mouse
And a humungous weta

Acknowledgements

Many people have freely offered help, information and photos for this book and I thank them all. There are so many helpful and obliging people out there who outweigh the other kind.

Because corrugated iron is so universal the sharing of its history was for the most part freely offered. Permission was granted from the Alexander Turnbull Library and the Army Museum to publish the photos credited on individual pages. Thanks also to New Zealand Steel, Pacific Coilcoaters, and the Department of Conservation for the photograph of the Camphouse.

Naming names risks leaving someone out, but a number of people made special contributions, particularly Sir John Ingram who generously wrote the foreword, and *subby* magazine editor Hugh Patterson (www.subby.co.nz) who had several key roles in getting the book into print.

Many contemporary architects incorporate corrugated iron in their work; we had great assistance from Nick Bevin and Ric Slessor. Nick wrote the thesis for his architecture degree in 1983 on the history and uses of the material.

Acknowledgement is due to the British Library for the publication of patent documents. Grateful thanks also to Peter Acland, John Aitchison, Margaret Bake, Shaun Barnett (blackrobin@xtra.co.nz; www.hedgehoghouse.com), Toby Bishop, Jocelyn Carlin (www.carlin.co.nz), Daisy Coles, Dave Collins, Brian Cosgrove, Dave Dulieu, Alistair Fleming, Alan Gapes, Alex Green, Tom Hayes, Terence Hodgson, Eleanor Holmes, Virginia King, Geoff Kirkham, Guthrun Love, Colin Martin, Bob Maysmor, Brendon Monaghan, John MacGibbon, my daughter Annie McNaught, John Miller, Lynn Peck, Margaret and Dave Segedin, John Southall, Simon Perris, Jeff Sparkes, my son Brian Thomson, Jeff Thomson (no relation!), my daughter Vivienne Thomson, Paul Thompson, Stephannie Tims, Gilbert van Reenen, Gerald Wagg, Roger Whelan, Antony Woodward and Jade Zhou ~ and special thanks to my very patient wife Alison.

ROBERT SMALL

Years ago when we were boys
We didn't have today's flash toys
A stick on a fence
Never made sense
But made great corrugated noise

Corrugated iron vied with asbestos (dirty word) sheeting as a popular cladding for the Kiwi bach or crib. The advent of the 40-hour week in the 1930s gave many Kiwis the chance to spend two days in seven away from home.

COLIN MARTIN PHOTOS

School's ended, excitement's growing
Children know where we're going
Mum's icing with almond paste
The Christmas cake, love the taste.

Pack the car, must get ready,
Find my togs, find my teddy
Inside the car the air's all thick
Gotta stop, my sister's sick.

There at last, open the door,
Familiar smells, sand on the floor
Fight breaks out, what a pain
Sister's claimed top bunk again.

So much swimming, so much fun
Coconut oil, soothes the sun
Shoulders have many blisters
Mine much worse than my sister's.

Christmas turkey, Christmas pud'
I wish I hadn't, don't feel too good
Was that Santa at the door?
I don't believe him any more.

Pretty hot, a roof of tin
Doesn't matter the state it's in
Ain't a Christmas that's a patch
On a Kiwi Christmas, in a Kiwi bach.

Right: Crib at Frankton, Queenstown
PAUL THOMPSON, ALEXANDER TURNBULL LIBRARY PA12 1336 08

From the furnaces & factories of Britain

The story of corrugated iron is closely associated with the Industrial Revolution and the rise of the British Empire. It was the right material at the right time.

Three factors led to its success. The first two were patents developed around the same time ~ one for corrugating and the other for galvanising iron sheets for roof and wall cladding.

The third factor was the exodus of migrants to the new colonies. The extent of Britain's 19th-century colonisation of the world used to be printed in red on every map. These colonies were new potential markets and had as much to do with corrugated iron's success as the product itself.

Who was first?

Just who invented corrugated iron is uncertain, as different parts of the production process were patented independently.

Henry Robinson Palmer is sometimes credited with inventing corrugated iron in London in 1829, but his patent No 5786 was for the use of corrugated iron as a roof and wall cladding, not for the machines that made it. He acknowledged that the method of corrugating by pressing was already well known. Palmer worked for the London Dock & Harbour Company, where he would have seen the potential of heavy gauge corrugated iron to cut down on the need for framing.

J & E Walker is believed to have been the first company to have actually made corrugated iron. John Walker was already advertising portable steel buildings clad in corrugated iron in 1832, so he must have been quick off the mark. By 1846 his firm's weekly production was 120 tons. The Walker family was heavily involved in the ironmaking business in England during the 18th and 19th century and had works in Islington (London), Derby, Chester, Newcastle and Liverpool. Samuel Walker had many sons but unfortunately called some of them Joshua, Joseph, Jonathon and John ~ all biblical names ~ so it is not easy to establish which J Walker was the one interested in corrugated iron.

In 1829 a corrugated iron patent (probably Palmer's) was bought by a Richard Walker of Rotherhithe, south-east London. Walker is another credited with making the first corrugated iron. It is not known if he was a relative of J & E Walker but he also had an ironworks in London and was exporting portable buildings from Bermondsey and Camberwell.

The first corrugating machines were slow and noisy. Heavy presses with a single curved die formed only one corrugation at a time. Samuel Parker in Auckland at the end of the 19th century, and EC Hayton of New Plymouth until the mid-20th century, both used this method of production in a press similar to that shown below.

There is another legend about the invention of corrugated iron. One day in the Phoenix Iron Works in West Bromwich, Birmingham, a sheet of metal serving as a guard protection for workers on a rail-making machine came loose and was pulled into the gears of the machine. It emerged thoroughly crunched into a series of waves. The workmen repaired the guard and got on with the job, but ironmaster John Spencer noticed the crumpled sheet and picked it up.

JOHN HEINE AND SON, LTD., SYDNEY, N.S.W.

A 1930s machinery catalogue shows a toggle press used for general pressing work, and often used to corrugate iron.

Klumpety thump, another corrugation
Klumpety thump, manual automation
Klumpety thump, more wrinkly tin
Klumpety thump, a helluva din
Klumpety thump,
Klumpety thump.

Instead of flopping around as a thin sheet of metal normally would, it remained rigid. Spencer stared at it. He stood it up and leaned his weight on it, but it didn't bend. Spencer stood still for several minutes ~ here was a marvellous new process which actually increased the strength of metal sheets! This discovery would revolutionise the building industry. Spencer lost no time in obtaining a patent and started corrugating sheets; other ironmasters soon followed his example.

Spencer's 1844 patent specification, No 10399, proposed corrugating iron by feeding sheets through a pair of longitudinally grooved matching rollers. This machine, a barrel corrugator, worked like two large gear wheels meshing together. Since Spencer had seen the guard being crunched he would naturally think of corrugating iron that way.

Neither the barrel method nor the die production method stretches the metal, but sheet width is reduced as each corrugation is formed. One advantage of corrugated sheets was that they could also be curved lengthwise. A roll-curving machine had three rolls; one above and two below, with grooved shafts similar to a plate-bending machine. Spencer included a curving machine in his patent and with these inventions effected a simple way to corrugate sheet metal and arch it for a curved roof at the same time.

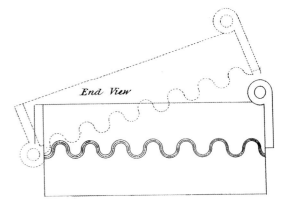

Nothing new under the sun: Morewood & Rogers did not pursue these two 1845 ideas ~ above, a press for corrugating iron; below, a roll-former which was 100 years before its time.

In 1845 Edmund Morewood and George Rogers' patent No 10859 proposed a different way to corrugate iron by passing the sheets progressively between a series of rolls shaped to the profile of the corrugations. Maybe they were trying to evade the Spencer patent; had they proceeded with this method, which is used universally today, they would have made the first roll-former.

The barrel method was the main way of corrugating iron before the manufacture of galvanised coil shortly before World War II, when roll-forming became the preferred method. Heavy machines could roll more than one light gauge sheet at a time, and barrel corrugators are still made and used in India. The Wellington branch of John Lysaght was using a (very noisy) barrel corrugator until the 1950s.

There is a big difference between how galvanised corrugated iron was manufactured then and now. Originally sheets were corrugated first, then galvanised; because long coils are now available we galvanise first and corrugate afterwards.

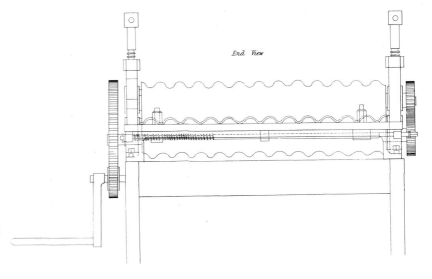

Corrugated iron was used in the United Kingdom during the 19th century for farm and industrial buildings and as roofing. It sometimes replaced thatch because it was cheap and easy to use, but never gained recognition as anything other than a temporary expedient. Ironically, corrugated iron is now regarded as a heritage material there.

Cast iron, wrought iron and steel

The iron that is corrugated has changed and been refined over the years.

A barrel corrugator was an efficient way to corrugate iron ~ but, like the press, the lengths were limited to the distance between the frames.

Iron ore is a common element which, when combined with other elements, makes three main types of iron: cast iron, wrought iron and steel. Although steel is now the most important, its production dates only from the 1850s, whereas cast and wrought iron processes have been known for thousands of years.

Cast and wrought iron are much more resistant to corrosion and rusting than steel. Cast iron, produced commercially after 1794, is smelted at a much higher temperature than wrought iron, and so becomes saturated with up to 5% carbon from the furnace fuel. This high carbon content means that it is rigid in compression, but weak in tension ~ it makes good columns, but dangerous beams! It is then cast into moulds to produce blocks. These castings are called 'pig iron' because the line of individual blocks connected to the pouring channel looks like a litter of suckling pigs.

It can be difficult to tell wrought from cast iron, but if you look at the end of a broken piece of wrought iron you see a fibrous structure, whereas a broken piece of cast iron is more crystalline and can be quite brittle. If you drop cast iron, it may break.

Wrought iron is smelted at a low temperature to produce a spongy mass of metal called a bloom, from which impurities are driven off as liquid slag. This process, known as puddling, involves hammering, hence 'worked' or 'wrought'. Wrought iron is very pure, with a carbon content of less than 1%. It is strong in tension and malleable, but labour-intensive to produce.

In the revolutionary Bessemer process for making steel, invented in 1856, air is blown through the molten metal, raising its temperature much higher than previous methods. The initial trial in the first Bessemer furnace at St Pancras, London, must have given Henry Bessemer and onlookers a few anxious moments ~ the reaction was so violent that it was ten minutes before the air could be turned off. During this process most of the impurities were burnt off and a malleable iron, named steel, was the result. Mild steel ~ the common name now used ~ is really wrought iron with the slag and impurities removed.

Notwithstanding this discovery, wrought iron rather than steel was used for corrugated iron until the late 1880s. Steel was regarded as inferior because phosphorus and other impurities were still present, and because it corroded more quickly than wrought iron.

For many centuries roofing metals in Europe had been non-ferrous ~ copper, lead and zinc. When wrought iron was used it had to be protected from rusting by a coating of tin, pitch or tar. Pressed tiles made from iron dipped in a bath of tin were used for roofing, but they were small and the lapping of their joints was not altogether satisfactory. The English firm Morewood & Rogers exported 3 foot x 2 foot Morewood pan roofing tiles to New Zealand ~ some were used at Port Nicholson and Nelson about 1853.

Because iron roofing sheets were much cheaper than copper and lead they were used on railway stations and dockyard buildings in a similar way to the traditional standing seam or batten roll which is still used with non-ferrous metals. This type of roofing was called 'pan roofing' and is known as 'fully supported' because it is not structural and requires support.

The great advantage of corrugated iron over flat pan iron was that the corrugations made it self-supporting, which reduced framing costs and made construction quicker and easier.

Galvanising

Zinc is an ancient metal. The Romans knew it as 'false silver', and a fountain partly covered with zinc was found in the ruins of Pompeii after its destruction in 79AD. The Chinese made coins of it in the 7th century and the English first heard about it from China. William Champion of Bristol obtained a patent for producing zinc in 1738. The method was known, not surprisingly, as the Bristol Process, and smelting began at Swansea in 1740.

Zinc was named by the Swiss chemist Theophrastus Bombastus von Hohenheim, who inspired the new Latin word *zincum*, which in English and French became *zinc*. We should be glad that zinc was not named after the chemist himself!

In a presentation to the French Royal Academy in 1742 chemist PJ Malouin described a method of coating iron by dipping it in molten zinc. Galvanised cooking pots were used in France in the ensuing years and zinc appeared as a roofing material in 1811, but was not in common use until the boom a few decades later.

In 1833 the English, Scotch & Irish Galvanised Metals Co was formed in London, and the following year patent rights for the Bristol Process were transferred to the British Galvanisation of Metals Co for a royalty of £3 per ton. Several other companies started up at this time.

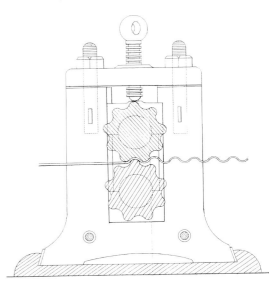

A.D.1844. Nov.R 23. Nº 10.399
SPENCER'S SPECIFICATION.

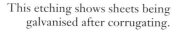

This etching shows sheets being galvanised after corrugating.

In 1837 Stanislaus Sorel, a French engineer, obtained a patent for a way to coat iron with zinc. It was called 'zincing on iron' and became known as galvanising. Sorel acknowledged the work of Galvani and Volta, who had discovered that electricity is generated through the contact of dissimilar metals ~ Volta had noticed that one of the two metals in his battery was always preserved from oxidation.

About this time industry was advancing rapidly, thanks to a new economic liberalism, and spurred on by the harnessing of energy that would develop the steam engine and soon transform manufacturing. England and France, who had led the world in producing tin plate, were at the forefront of galvanising. The same year Sorel received a French patent, Commander HV Craufurd of the Royal Navy was awarded an English patent for a similar process, no doubt derived from Sorel's. His was for the galvanic preservation of iron by cleaning it with sulphuric acid and fluxing it (a process which promotes fusion) with ammonium chloride, then completely covering the metal surface by dipping it in a bath of molten zinc. The next few years saw numerous patent infringement squabbles, from which ensued the inevitable litigation.

To galvanise iron, sheets were cut to length, corrugated, placed in a cradle and lowered into a bath of pure zinc. Cleaning and fluxing ensured that a thin molecular alloy layer formed to bond the thicker zinc to the iron. Molten zinc was drained off and the sheets were shaken, lowered into hot water and wiped dry. Because galvanising was done manually the process was slow and crude, but in this way the galvanised corrugated iron industry was born.

Morewood & Rogers' 1845 patent described a different way of galvanising by 'tinning the steel' with copper, tin or other metals before dipping it into the zinc bath. Were they trying to get around a patent again?

By 1850 the British galvanising industry was using 10,000 tons of zinc a year to protect iron. Zinc is now the world's most commonly used metal after iron, aluminium and copper.

In 1888 the first four-roll galvanising machine was developed in John Lysaght's Bristol factory, but its sheet pots were not fully mechanised and the machine didn't provide an even coating of zinc. Variation in thickness was sometimes caused by the way the alloy developed as the sheets were racked for cooling, or because the exit rolls at the bottom of the pot became misaligned and removed more zinc from the underside of the sheets.

The life expectancy of galvanised iron depends on the environment and the thickness of the coating, rather than the iron itself. When the zinc weathers away, the iron oxidises and becomes red with rust.

Early sheets were rolled with eight symmetrical corrugations to allow two side laps. In New Zealand it became common to give only one and a half laps, which meant turning over alternate sheets. This resulted in a checkerboard effect when one side corroded more than the other.

Pure zinc is a brittle metal and if the coating is too thick when the sheet is galvanised it cracks on the bends. This microcracking is not as bad as it seems because the zinc still offers protection, as Faraday discovered in 1829. Where the coating is cracked or cut, the zinc will corrode instead of the iron in a process called *sacrificial* or *cathodic protection*. Other metals do not protect steel like this. Tin, the other metal commonly used, works in reverse. It is not sacrificial to the steel base, acting only as a barrier. If a tin can is scratched, the iron underneath corrodes because it becomes sacrificial to the tin. Thus tin cans thrown outside rust quickly even though they have a lacquer protection.

Plating

A galvanised roof is not a 'tin roof' ~ it is neither made of tin nor coated with it. The use of the word 'tin' may have come about because tin plate and galvanising look similar. The term 'tin

On some older buildings the uneven coating came about because every alternate sheet was turned over.

Possums and cats
Seagulls and rats
They fight and they mate
The racket they make
Keeps me awake.
Why congregate
On my corrugate?

Tadeusz Sendzimir, who developed continuous rolling mills.
WWW.SENDZIMIR.COM

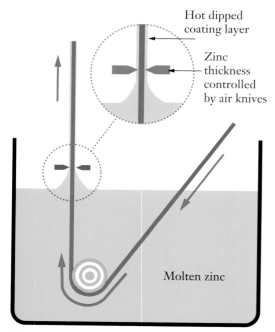

Hot dipped coating layer

Zinc thickness controlled by air knives

Molten zinc

The modern way of galvanising, using steel coil.

roof' has been so widely and affectionately used for so long that any crusade to correct it would fail.

One roof cladding material ~ Terne plate ~ does actually have a tin coating (one part tin to three parts lead). *Terne* in French means dull.

The term 'plate' also has many meanings and may confuse. As a noun it can be anything thin and flat, or a thin layer upon another surface (e.g. gold plating). As a verb it usually refers to the method, as in tin plating, zinc plating or electroplating. Tin plating can now be done by hot-dipping or electroplating. Zinc deposited electrolytically is known as electroplated. Dipping iron into a bath of molten zinc is termed galvanising and dipping it into molten tin is called tinning. Still confused?

Advanced coating methods

Continuous rolling mills were invented around 1937 by a Polish engineer, Tadeusz Sendzimir, who had emigrated to the United States. These mills changed the galvanising coating process dramatically, by producing continuous lengths from steel coils welded or stitched together. Prior to this technology, zinc coating was much thicker than it is now ~ about 800g/m² (grams per square metre) compared with today's 450 g/m².

By the 1950s in the UK, and in the 1960s worldwide, most steel mills had converted to the new process. Zinc was now applied continuously before sheets were corrugated.

The batch pot method was replaced with totally mechanised galvanising lines that coat steel coil evenly. When the coil leaves its zinc bath, air-jet 'knives' accurately measure and control the amount of zinc left on it.

Because the zinc coating process was continuous and the coating could be better controlled than with dipping, the industry agreed to a coating thickness of 1.25 ounces per square foot (380g/m²). This was the standard from 1950 until 1970, when the coating thickness for corrugated iron and other profiles and rainwater goods (spouting and downpipes) was upped by agreement to 1.75 ounces per square foot (534g/m²). The thickness did drop back to 400g/m² for a period and now the standard coating weight for plain unpainted galvanised coil and sheet for roof and wall cladding is 450g/m². The reason given for this change was that the control and evenness of the coating process had improved, but the skyrocketing price of zinc might have had an influence!

Much confusion exists when comparing products made from sheet and coil with those that are hot-dipped after being fabricated, because the thickness of the zinc coating is described in both cases in grams per square metre. The thickness on roof and wall cladding refers to the collective amount on both sides of the sheet, effectively dividing the coating weight by half. It is therefore misleading to compare the coating weight of hot-dipped zinc on nails, screws or fabricated products with that on sheet and coil.

It is also inaccurate to compare it with the coating weight of the aluminium/zinc coating mostly used for corrugated iron in New Zealand since 1994 because aluminium is only a third as heavy as zinc. In 1994 a decision was made by BHP New Zealand Steel to introduce a new pot in the galvanising line to coat steel with a mixture of aluminium and zinc, rather than pure zinc. This was a patented process with the tradename Zincalume.

Coatings are now described both by the material and the weight in g/m^2, e.g. Z450 and AZ150.

The thickness of the aluminium/zinc alloy standard coating used for corrugated cladding is $150g/m^2$ and is called AZ150, although an optional thickness of AZ200 was introduced into New Zealand in 2003. An AZ150 coating is approximately the same thickness (.04mm both sides) as Z275 zinc ($275g/m^2$) because for an equal thickness an AZ coating has approximately half the weight of a Z coating.

This coating thickness on each side of the steel is one quarter the thickness of the paper you are reading from.

Weight of zinc 7150 g/m^2 = 1mm thickness

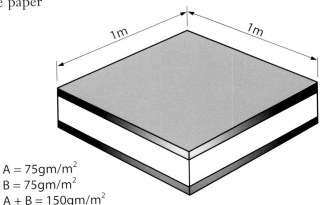

A = 75gm/m^2
B = 75gm/m^2
A + B = 150gm/m^2

Coating	g/m²	mm	μ	μ each side
Z	450	.063	63	32
Pre-painted steel	275	.038	38	19
AZ	150	.038	38	19

A micron (μ) is one thousandth of a millimetre.
Although other coating thicknesses are available, these are the most commonly used for corrugated roof and wall cladding.

New Zealand Steel's galvanising line at Glenbrook shows the continuous coil 'dipping' into a bath of molten zinc which solidifies on its upward path.
NEW ZEALAND STEEL

The roar is muffled to a hum
But soon forgotten
When in the theatre
We witness a birth.

A steely mundane coil
Instantly transformed
To a shimmering silver ribbon
Disappearing upwards.

Gone from sight
But yet to reappear
As a respected member of society
Coloured or corrugated.
The wonder
Of such metamorphosis.

Prefabricated buildings

In the early days of corrugated iron, prefabricated buildings were developed in London, Bristol and Manchester. In 1821 Richard Walker built a factory in Bermondsey, London, as an open-ended warehouse, with a barrel-vaulted roof using curved iron sheets riveted together and lateral tie rods. He built several similar sheds at the London docks and one at the gasworks at Vauxhall around 1837. Heavy gauge corrugated iron meant that the buildings could be virtually frameless.

By the late 1840s Edward Bellhouse, a leading Manchester engineer, was making prefabricated buildings. ET Bellhouse & Co became the major supplier to the gold rush sites of California in 1849 ~ their buildings could be packaged and transported easily to fulfil the urgent need for housing. A two-roomed cottage cost less than £100 ~ a two-storey eight-roomed house would set you back nearly £500. Corrugated buildings were also in demand when gold fever hit Australia in Ballarat in 1851. Bellhouse found other outlets: in England he sold tenant farmers buildings they could disassemble so as not to form part of the squire's freehold; to Brazil and Chile he sold railway buildings.

At the Great Exhibition at Crystal Palace in 1851 Bellhouse displayed a model emigrants' cottage that could go out to the colonies on the same ship as the emigrant family.

Prince Albert, a prime instigator of the Great Exhibition, saw the potential of Bellhouse's prefabricated buildings and promptly ordered one himself. Balmoral Castle was being built at this time and was not likely to be finished for five years. Albert wanted an instant ballroom, dining room and theatre. He ordered a 60 x 24 foot building from Bellhouse with horizontal corrugated iron cladding ~ it was delivered to Inverness by train a few weeks later. The Bellhouse building was used until the castle was completed in 1856 and it is still in use today as a joiner's shop.

Prince Albert's ballroom by Bellhouse.

Prince Albert was not the only royal to use corrugate: King Eyambo of Nigeria is said to have built for himself (and his 320 wives) a palace at Calabar clad with corrugated iron.

Bellhouse's early prefabricated cottages were clad with flat iron whereas his two-storey buildings used corrugated iron, protected with a tin alloy that gave the appearance of frosted silver. By the 1850s Bellhouse had changed the design of all his cottages so that their galvanised corrugated cladding ran vertically and their curved roofs became pitched.

The Crystal Palace exhibition also showcased what manufacturers could provide for independent railway companies, notably prefabricated station buildings which could be delivered directly to site by rail. When it was only painted and not galvanised, however, exhaust steam and gases from locomotives corroded the iron.

By 1853 Samuel Hemming of Bristol was offering prefabricated buildings ranging from churches to shops and houses, and his company had established a good market in Australia and New Zealand (see etching opposite).

In 1853 the first kitset do-it-yourself buildings were exported from Edinburgh by Charles Young, who by this time was also prefabricating iron structures including railway stations, storage buildings and residences.

The prepackaged portable building market boomed until the 1900s, by which time the gold rushes were over. Economic prosperity meant that people had extra money to spend on their homes, and they spent it on luxury and adornment rather than wrinkly tin, to show the neighbours that they too had 'made it'.

A corrugated iron cottage (in Australia), constructed according to the patented system of Edward Bellhouse of Manchester.

When the Brits sailed away from their home
To start a new life out here
They had some idea what they wanted
But how to, wasn't too clear

The first thing of greatest importance
Was to erect for themselves a small house
And though they were perfectly willing
They brought tools but not enuf nous

Some bought a deal that was packaged
Some had an idea 'twas worth tryin'
Some wanted a little square box
Just made out of corrugated iron

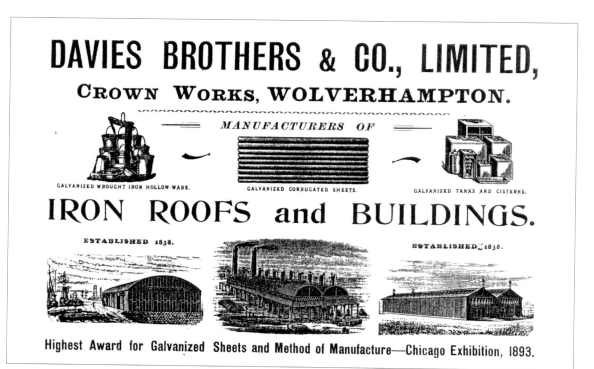

Prefabricated churches were convenient because congregations fluctuated as people moved from place to place. These 'tin tabernacles' came in different sizes and cost roughly £1 per head ~ you could purchase a 300-seat church for £300.

A Hemming prefab ~ the colonial idyll.

It's hard to know what they hoped
Or what was in the mind
Of those who packed their hammocks
Not knowing what they would find

It's hard to know what they felt
On the long voyage at sea
Whether they would be better off
Four months just to wait and see.

It's hard to know what they saw
As the first land came into view
All those hills and mountains
And all that forest too

It's hard to know what they did,
And how they established their claim
But to build a bit of a shelter ~
That was the name of the game.

It is not hard to imagine their feelings
They'd surely be highly elated
To sleep their very first sleep
In their shed that was all corrugated.

Iron & Wooden Houses.

NOW LANDING, EX "INVINCIBLE,"
HEMMING'S
Patent Improved Portable Buildings,
CLIFT HOUSE, BRISTOL.

FOUR STORES, 25 x 37 x 12 feet,
One ditto, 25 x 36 x 12 feet,
Two SHOPS, 24 x 33 x 9 feet, with three Apartments behind, and with mahogany Counter and Shelves, complete,
Two HOUSES, 26 · 6 x 14 feet, with 5 rooms each,
One HOUSE, 26 x 22 feet, with 4 rooms, passage, closets, &c.

The Frame-work of the above Buildings consists of Iron and Timber, the Sills of Oak. The walls and roof are of galvanised corrugated Iron. The walls are lined with ½-inch boarding, covered with canvass, ready for papering, leaving a space of 4½ inches throughout the entire building between the iron and wood work, by which means a complete ventilation is effected, and the temperature in Summer much lessened, and increased in Winter. The doors have 4 pannels, with good locks and hinges, and the sashes are glazed with glass

'The Stables', near Martinborough
on the south coast of the Wairarapa.
TODD FYFE

A timber roof or wall is greatly stiffened by
corrugated iron cladding, as any builder knows.
ELEANOR HOLMES

There was an old shed in Waipatiki
That always seemed a bit rickety
But cyclone Bola
Bowled it all over
Repairing it would be trickity-dickity

The market Down Under

In New Zealand, Australia and South America, initial reluctance to use the wrinkly roofing was soon overcome when settlers discovered its versatility. Though regarded as a temporary expedient, it was cheap compared with other cladding, convenient to transport, easy to handle, quick to put up and quicker to pull down. Its comparative light weight and the corrosion protection offered by the zinc coating made the product ideal for mining towns, army barracks and housing. It was suitable for roofing because our climate is milder than the Brits were used to, notwithstanding the heat of the sun in the day and the chill of the night frost. They happily clad walls in corrugated iron, but did attempt to insulate them with leaves and newspapers.

Corrugated iron may not have made such an impression in the UK or Europe, but in the colonies it was just the product the settlers needed, and its ready-made market expanded with every immigrant ship.

By 1843 Englishman John Porter was producing and exporting corrugated iron to Hong Kong, Ceylon and the West Indies. As it had with prefabricated buildings, the 1851 gold rush in Australia gave a great impetus to his exports of this 'universal material'.

Engineers liked the material because it gained strength from corrugating and its symmetrical profile could be easily curved for roofs and made into tanks, conveyor covers and self-supporting shelters.

In 1857 a young Irishman, John Lysaght, acquired a small galvanising business in Bristol. He turned his attention to the galvanising and corrugating of sheet iron and began exporting his Orb brand to the rural and building markets in Australia and New Zealand. By 1900 three-quarters of Lysaght's corrugated iron was exported to Australia and in 1918 they set up a company there.

In 1920 the UK steel conglomerate GKN (Guest, Keen & Nettlefold) bought John Lysaght UK, and the next year John Lysaght started its own plant in Australia and took over the Orb brand.

John Lysaght pioneered production of corrugated iron in the United Kingdom and eventually dominated the Antipodes.
LIGHTMOOR PRESS (WWW.LIGHTMOOR.CO.UK)

The advertiser's claim that iron would never rust or need painting was in the same league as the claim that houses built from it would be fireproof. 'Mosewood' is a misspelling of Morewood.

The Auckland daily *Southern Cross* regularly advertised corrugated iron for the settlers.

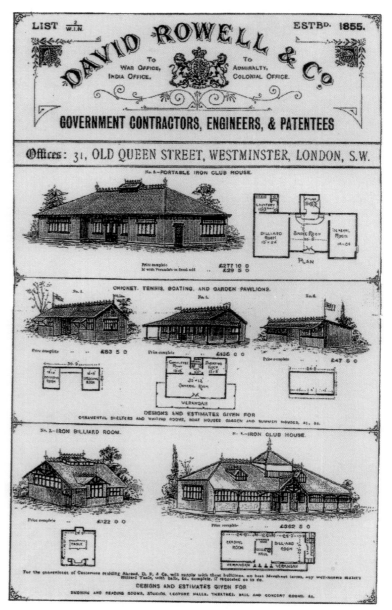

Auctions and orders

Sheet consignments from Britain were sold either from the warehouse or by auction, even though this gamble could result in a loss. In 1857 Auckland's daily *Southern Cross* advertised six tons of 6-foot corrugated iron sheets for sale and the next year there were twenty tons of 6, 7 and 8-foot sheets on offer. The cost of a 6-foot sheet was approximately one shilling. Today the same sheet would set you back $17.

In 1862 fifteen cases of various thicknesses were put up for sale, and Connell & Ridlings were offering Morewood & Rogers and Tupper & Co's Anchor brand 8-foot sheets curved for verandahs. Their claim that it would never rust or need painting was in the same league as the claim that houses made from it would be fireproof. Forty tons of coal and a 'very superior' fire brigade are offered for sale in the same paper!

Tupper & Co from the UK placed regular advertisements in the *Southern Cross*. There was also a brisk trans-Tasman trade where entrepreneurs were on-selling UK materials from Australia. Shorter sheets were preferred because they fitted easily into horse-drawn drays or could be strapped to the side of a packhorse.

By 1894 British exports of galvanised iron had grown to an amazing 170,000 tons, of which Australia took 41,700 tons. New Zealand's requirements were 5, 6, 7, 8, 9 and 10-foot lengths, bought for just over £11 per ton. South Africa, India, Argentina and Chile were the other main importers.

Gauging the thickness

Material was ordered by gauge ~ the thickness measurement. This was Birmingham Gauge (BG), as distinct from Standard Wire Gauge (SWG) which was (and still is) used for non-ferrous metals. BG 26g was .018 inch (.45mm) but the canny New Zealanders, maybe those with Scottish ancestry, thought they could save a few pounds by ordering thinner steel. Thus it happened that there were two '26' gauges, one for this country and one for the rest of the world. Our 26g was euphemistically called '26g commercial', but was 20% thinner than standard.

Following the advent of continuous rolling the thickness of corrugated iron has been measured as the base metal thickness (BMT) without the coating. Since metrication in 1964, two thicknesses have been commonly used: .40mm (28g), and .55mm (25g). Even today our thinnest corrugated roof cladding is thinner than Australia's, where they use .45mm (27g)

Tametekapua meeting house at Ohinemutu, Rotorua. Māori quickly adopted corrugated iron for their whare, storehouses and meeting houses. Painted in the traditional red, they are a distinctive feature of the Aotearoa environment.
OWEN HOWARD

and .60mm (24g). New Zealand's frugality has now been well surpassed by the south-east Asian countries, who use .019mm (35g) ~ paper-thin stuff that only cats can walk on.

Fortunately the corrosion performance of galvanised iron depends on the coating, not the steel base thickness.

The colonial climate

To understand the settlers' motivation and their love affair with corrugated iron, it helps to understand what sort of people they were and the circumstances of their times.

Edward Jerningham Wakefield (Edward Gibbon Wakefield's son) sailed out to New Zealand with 35 others on the 382-ton barque *Tory* which arrived at Port Nicholson (Wellington) in September 1839. The voyage was usually about 120 days but with favourable winds the *Tory* took only 96 ~ a record. The young Wakefield spent four years 'colonising' for the New Zealand Land Company before returning home. He came here again in 1850 on the *Lady Nugent*.

In 1848 he wrote a booklet offering *Advice to intending colonists*. Excerpts follow:

> It will not, perhaps, be thought impertinent to the object of this work, to point out to the intending colonist of what preparations he stands in need. It has not been uncommon for persons to engage in colonisation who were totally devoid of the slightest knowledge, not only of the country to which they were going, but of what it was necessary to take with them, and of what they would have to do on their arrival.
>
> When the first Colonists went to the settlements in Cook's Strait, they took with them many wooden houses which had been constructed in England, so as to take to pieces, pack and be put together again on landing. This was a necessary precaution on arriving in a land where there was sure to be no sawn timber ready for them. At the present time, [1848] however, there are numerous sawmills at all the existing settlements, which supply excellent building timber at lower prices than it can be carried out from England; and the cost of labour in erecting the house is very little more in one case than the other. It is well to take out all kinds of fixtures required for fitting a house, a small stock of firebricks, fire-grates, dogs for wood-fires, kitchen-ranges, stoves, boilers, &c., and some corrugated iron or zinc will be found very handy for roofing houses or verandahs quickly.
>
> It is also worth the Colonists' while to look at the iron houses made for exportation by Cottam and Hallam, Oxford-street.

Opposite: Hut in the Haast area, West Coast. If you're making the rest of the building out of corrugated iron, why not the chimney too?

This photo's a scene from the past
A pioneers' hut in the Haast
Its chimney of tin
Used to keep the smoke in
I bet that OSH is aghast.

In winter a little tin house
Let in the cold quite a lotta
But then when the summer came later
It got hotta and hotta and hotta.

The answer came as they do
And it made the house a lot grander
A Kiwi spectacular vernacular
The corrugate bullnosed verandah!

The houses of South Street in Nelson have been converted to boutique B&Bs within walking distance of the city centre.
COLIN MARTIN

The popularity of corrugated iron can be seen by this recommendation, yet it had only been available for a few years. In his book *The Britain of the South* Charles Hursthouse also recommends "some corrugated iron roofing stuff, iron rod and wire for porch or verandah."

Many settlers had left the UK because they saw no future there, without jobs and unable to pay rent. With nothing to lose, anywhere would be better than where they were, alongside Britain's 'Satanic mills'. Blake's words in the hymn 'Jerusalem' referred to the cotton, woollen, and steel mills, and how "England's green and pleasant land" was being desecrated by the smog and smoke from such factories.

Most emigrants were adventurous spirits who longed for a change and a challenge. The New Zealand Company intended to perpetuate class distinctions, so those who could afford it paid their way, while the 'labouring types' had free passage.

The Company's method of attracting investors and colonists encouraged speculation and absentee ownership, deterring genuine farmers and creating immense problems. Some buyers remained comfortably in England, aiming to profit from the allocation of 'town acres' which they could subdivide and sell or rent to merchants near the wharf or the main streets, or sell as residential sections. There was an imbalance between labour and capital in settlements, as insufficient buyers emigrated to provide work for the labourers and few genuine farmers were prepared to buy unseen land.

The new arrivals were a varied lot; some arrived with nothing, others had substantial resources. Those lucky enough to have money could obtain land by ballot (or by the spinning of a lottery wheel) from the New Zealand Company. Some of those who finally did emigrate became landed gentry. The land allocation varied from place to place. In Port Nicholson it was 101 acres: one town acre and 100 country acres.

Among the 'lower class' labourers were builders who brought skills with them, but the big lure for all immigrants was the land. For the first time in their lives labourers could have their very own piece of dirt and build a home. No matter how modest this was, it was a realisable dream if they worked hard and helped one another. The land was only worth its cost if there was a use for it. Hence in the early 1850s flat land in the parish of Pakuranga was worth £1 an acre, whereas hilly land in the parish of Karangahape was worth only half that amount. Australia was comparatively cheaper at 5 shillings an acre and Dunedin dearer at £2 an acre.

Land disputes arose almost immediately. The New Zealand Company claimed to have purchased 20 million acres but on occasion had not enquired into the bona fides of the Māori people prepared to sell. Pakeha and Māori were understandably concerned about land sales and settlers blamed both the government and the Company, who then engaged in mutual recrimination. It was not long, however, before Māori found the Pakeha 'wrinkly tin' a quick and easy way to thatch a pā or pātaka (food house).

Settlers in Dunedin, Wanganui, Port Nicholson and Nelson had a shock in store when they arrived. Much of the land was not flat and had not really been surveyed, but was divided by straight lines without regard for topography. Some of the land could not be built on and eventually many town acres were cut into four, providing the Kiwi quarter-acre. Unfortunately the division was often made with narrow road frontages and this in turn decided the shape of the houses and their roofs. Some two-storey houses in Aro Street and Tinakori Road in Wellington are on narrow sections where corrugated iron was used on the walls because of the proximity of the next house, in the vain hope that it would make them fireproof.

South Street in Nelson is New Zealand's oldest entire street of original houses still standing. In spite of extensive renovation they are still essentially as they were when built. This was 'Townacre 456', bought in 1851 from the New Zealand Company, and No 13 was the first built, in 1863. It is not known how much of the corrugated iron is original but some of it is very old, as the brands show.

What the new settlers were in for may be seen in Edward Wakefield's book:

> There are three ways of taking out capital to the colony:
>
> 1. Take gold. This is probably the best way of all. Pack your sovereigns in a strong wooden box, and pay freight and insurance upon them.
>
> 2. Pay the money into the Union Bank of Australia, No. 38, Old Broad-street, City. This Bank has so complete a monopoly of the interchange of money between England and the colony, that its other charges are equally exorbitant.
>
> [There is no mention of the third way.]
>
> The length of the voyage is on an average 120 days and as no water is allowed for washing clothes, it is necessary to provide a sufficient stock of linen for this time. By stowing away in canvas bags that which has been used, and occasionally airing it on deck in fine weather, much of it may be preserved for washing on arrival, and subsequent use in the bush.
>
> It is almost needless to recommend as much exercise, on deck, as the weather will allow. If you want a good saltwater bath, remember that, except in very rough weather, the

Fireproofed by corrugate? Houses in Tinakori Road, and below, the Thistle Hotel, Wellington.

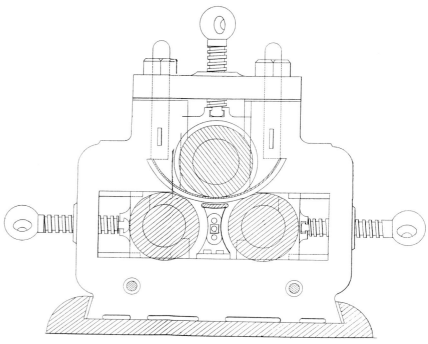

No. 55H. HAND CORRUGATED CURVING ROLLERS.

Left and above: This 1930 John Heine & Son machinery catalogue shows the pyramid curving machine that hasn't changed since Spencer's 1844 patent diagram.

This machine rolls water tanks
And curves as you can see
It's slowly turned by two old cranks
The other one is me

Opposite: Corrugated walls and frontages in Egmont Street, Wellington, early 20th century.

decks are washed at sunrise, or soon after, every morning. So go on deck in a bathing-dress, and let the sailors throw pails of water over you.

The colonist should learn how to bleed, set a broken or dislocated limb, and bind wounds. If he can even learn how to amputate a limb, so much the better.

By all means learn how to shoe a horse.

Needless to say, people of this kind would have no difficulty in nailing up a few sheets of corrugated iron.

To attract suitable types of people to the colony, free passage was offered to those who were deemed to be "mechanics able to do country work", including "Cartwrights, Sawyers and Bricklayers." One can imagine what they thought when their pay turned out to be one shilling and sixpence per day for single men and two shillings and sixpence a day for married men, and their first accommodation was in a Maori raupo hut at six shillings per week!

Away from the settled areas tents were used, and later square gable-ended corrugated iron huts were built and nicknamed 'tin tents'. Although brick was considered a safe building material in the UK, it was the opposite in New Zealand ~ the earthquakes of 1848 and 1855 must have frightened the wits out of the settlers. Moreover, it was logical to use timber for framing because trees were at hand. Some buildings were timber-clad, but nothing could compare with the ease of corrugated iron. The habit of building a fireplace into the structure, framing the chimney with timber and cladding it with corrugated iron was not a bright idea. The use of raupo or other thatch led inevitably to a number of disastrous fires, one of which occurred in Wellington in 1842. Such fires, however, did show the value of metal-clad buildings compared to those roofed with shingles, raupo, nikau or toetoe. By 1858, 80% of the 13,000 houses in the new colony were timber-framed, mostly with corrugated iron roofs, and insurance companies were offering reduced premiums on metal-roofed houses.

Corrugated iron cost much less than alternatives. With shingles at 15 shillings per thousand plus scantlings at 14 shillings per hundred feet, the

Colonial cottages.

Bay villa.

cost of a shingle roof was fourpence per square foot, but only one penny for 26g corrugated iron.

The alternative of using timber shingles for roofing instead of corrugated iron was not such a good idea either. Untreated timber shingles exposed to the elements only lasted ten years compared with 50 or more for corrugated iron. Often leaky shingle roofs were reroofed with corrugated iron, leaving the shingles in place.

Early design

The design of cottages, and later villas, was largely determined by the timber construction and the lightweight corrugated iron roofing material. The basic one-room cottage was only about 16 feet wide, but could expand with the growth of the family or when the pocket allowed.

It was easy to duplicate another gable alongside it or to add one at right angles. In each case a valley and an internal gutter was required. This probably stretched the do-it-yourself capability of the owner, who found it easier to add a lean-to onto the original gable-ended house at the back, or perhaps on all three sides with a verandah on the front. Over time the pioneers developed a style that is now distinctive.

The verandah was a common add-on to early cottages. Later it became a part of the original design, starting below the eaves of the main house. Rainwater from the verandah was taken to a separate tank or else it had no spouting at all.

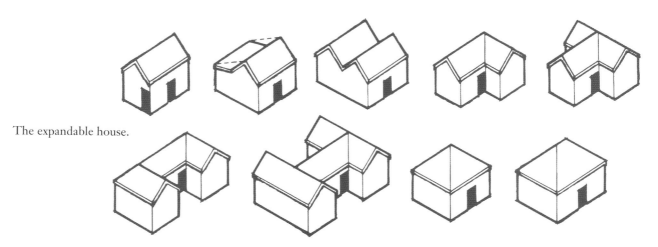

The expandable house.

The original 45° roof pitch on houses was a carry-over from Britain where snow is common and slates and tiles require a steep pitch to be weatherproof. 45° made for easy calculations!

Californian bungalow & Spanish Mission

The pitch of corrugated iron did not have to be so high for drainage and over the years settlers gradually reduced it. When the bungalow-style house arrived from California in the 1920s the pitch lowered to about 20° and when the Spanish Mission style came in the 1930s and the roof was hidden by a parapet, it came down drastically to 5°.

Verandahs that in some cases went right round the house were a welcome shelter from the weather, and became a show of affluence. Some original houses had striped canvas awnings. When these were mimicked in curved corrugated iron they also painted them in stripes, often in red and white or buff. Shopfront verandahs are still a strong New Zealand street tradition.

Californian bungalow.

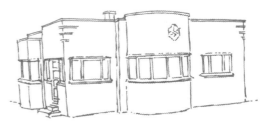

Spanish Mission.

Curved verandahs on Queen Street, Auckland.
TERENCE HODGSON

Above: The Newman house in Opunake, with
its concave corrugated verandah striped to
mimic the canvas awnings it replaced.
Margaret Segedin

Left: The bullnosed verandah on this Te Kuiti
house is enhanced by cast iron trim.
Terence Hodgson collection

There is, we're told, no choice as to who our parents are
Fate, it is said, dictates
There is a choosing though
Of what happens between life's certainties of birth and death
To shelter others on the journey, and give comfort to many,
To share a love with but a few
To give laughter,
To do so with unnoticed humility

Colonists who still longed for home sometimes imitated stone in wood at their house corners, and ornate timber fretwork at verandah posts or gables was reminiscent of the cast-iron lacework they had left behind.

The house at 128 Tasman Street, Opunake, built in 1887 by the Newman family (also known as the Feaver house) shows the striped verandahs that copied the canvas ones they replaced, and mimics stone corners with timber and paint. In 1983 this house was bought by my daughter Ann and her husband. They have restored it, including the bay window, the stained-glass windows and the concave verandah roof.

Refinements appeared ~ two-storey houses became popular, followed by the dormer window and later the bay window which really set a house apart from its neighbours. These additions required skills, some of which were homegrown. Versatile tradesmen curved the timber supporting structure for convex corrugated iron verandahs. The bullnosed verandah appeared when cottages were upgraded to villas during the 1880s, and later a double reverse curve verandah sheet appeared. This shape echoed the prevalent OG (Old Gothic) galvanised spouting, sometimes called Old Grecian or Colonial ~ see the drawing on this page.

Often the front of the house was a façade of timber weatherboards while the other three walls were clad with corrugated iron that was hoped to be fire protection because of the proximity to the neighbours. The plans were simple so that the roof structure was easy to build. The walls of the passage down the middle of the house supported the relatively lightweight roof structure required for corrugated iron roofing and the kitchen or bathroom (if any) enabled any wastewater to be disposed of out the back.

The long-drop, of course, was made from sheets of corrugate bent around the corners. Corrugated iron water tanks collected the water ~ tinsmiths must have been busy!

The population explosion greatly increased the demand for corrugated iron in New Zealand during the 19th century. The growth in the Pākehā population was spectacular:

1843 – 13,000
1850 – 26,000
1860 – 80,000
1870 – 248,000
1880 – 485,000

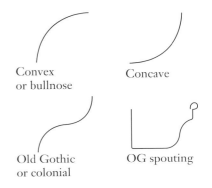

Convex or bullnose   Concave

Old Gothic or colonial   OG spouting

The judge's dunny at the Nelson Law Courts, circa 1957.
LES CLEVELAND

Alberton, Mt Albert, Auckland. This romantic timber mansion began as a farmhouse in 1863 and was later expanded to 18 rooms, with fairytale decorative verandahs and towers. It is now a museum.
Hugh Patterson

Our oldest iron

The earliest examples of imported galvanised corrugated iron has been found on farm buildings in Matanaka, near Waikouaiti in Otago. The stables, granary and schoolhouse were roofed in 1843 with Morewood & Rogers 'patent galvanised tinned iron'.

Alberton, the historic homestead in Auckland built in 1863, was also roofed with Morewood & Rogers-branded Gospel Oak. When it was repaired recently the zinc on the underside of the iron was found to have twice the thickness of today's coating.

The Camphouse on the slopes of Mt Taranaki is our oldest corrugated prefabricated building and came originally from Victoria, Australia. It was built on Marsland Hill in New Plymouth in 1856 as part of the military barracks and was used by the militia during the land wars. In 1891 it was shifted by sled to its present location at the end of the North Egmont Road. It has a half-round roof and the original iron on the walls, but the roof has blown off twice since then. The walls, made with 1.15mm (18g) galvanised iron, are still in excellent condition and have rifle firing slits ~ loopholes ~ from the wars. It is probable that this heavy material was curved in the factory and shipped to Australia as cladding for the many prefabricated buildings

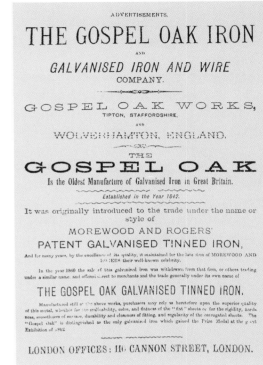

Matanaka farm buildings in Otago are New Zealand's oldest surviving farm buildings. Their corrugated iron roofing was made by Morewood & Rogers, who had not long begun manufacture in Great Britain. The buildings include a stable, storehouse, granary, schoolhouse and privy, and were built for whaler and merchant Johnny Jones.
MURRAY THOMSON

The Camphouse on Mt Taranaki, New Zealand's oldest corrugate-clad building, now serves as a DoC hut.
DEPARTMENT OF CONSERVATION/NOELENE TAYLOR

sent there. A distance away from the salt air and in one of New Zealand's most 'well washed' areas, and preserved with numerous coats of paint, the material is in excellent condition and is probably among the oldest corrugated iron in use in the world today. The Department of Conservation is proud of this building, which has been on the mountain for over a hundred years and still provides accommodation. It is easily the oldest building in any of our national parks.

A highly visible 'corrugated hut on stilts' is the Colonial Ammunition Company shot tower in Mt Eden, Auckland, built in 1916 and on the register of the New Zealand Historic Places Trust. Shot towers were the late 18th-century invention of English plumber William Watts, who noticed that raindrops were not shaped like teardrops but like spheres. By dripping molten lead through a sieve from above, perfectly round lead shot was produced which solidified as it fell into a water-filled pit at its base.

There once was a shot-maker, Fred
Who worked in a polygon shed
He was not on the ground
But heavenly bound
Up a hundred-rung ladder instead

Fred made a lot of lead shot
Some say he deserved what he got
But one thing's for sure
He had much to endure
When his tin shed got right bloody hot

It probably wouldn't suit me
He must have been out of his tree
Though the outlook was stunning
In the absence of plumbing
He wisely never drank tea

The settlers brought religion with them, and churches were among their first buildings. As well as the portable prefabricated ones they built a number that are still in use today, and all have corrugated iron roofs. Some have been reroofed, but generally they are much the same as they were 150 years ago. Westney Road Methodist Church in Mangere opened in 1856 and had lead on its roof taken by Māori to make bullets.

Not far away on Kirkbride Road, Mangere, was the Presbyterian church built in 1874 for £220. The photo shows the present minister to be one Rev. R Christian!

Another one-time 'country' church, St Pauls ~ built in 1886 ~ is on Chapel Road, East Tamaki, Auckland. Although still in use it probably will not last much longer ~ suburbia is closing in. Christ Church in Alfriston Road, Auckland, was built in 1877 at a cost of £146, about the same cost as the prefab churches that were marketed at £1 a seat.

British-style structural brick construction was used for both domestic and commercial building in the 19th century but proved a death trap for those caught in the Napier earthquake in 1931. It was not used subsequently. The bracing effect corrugated cladding gave roofs and walls was well known by settlers, and was clearly demonstrated at the disastrous mudslide at Abbotsford in Dunedin in 1979 when 69 houses were destroyed. Only those with corrugated roofs were relatively in one piece when they came to rest at the bottom of the slide.

The Presbyterian church on Kirkbride Road, Mangere, Auckland was built in 1874. Many similar early churches are still in use today.

Our vicar, the Reverend Wynne
Specialised in Original Sin
His church, we are told
Was centuries old
And its roof was original tin

Taranaki scene.
ANNIE McNAUGHT

When you speed along the highway
and catch a glimpse of an old farm house
Do you see years of neglect
or do you see a home that was once proud?
Do you hear the rattle of loose iron on the roof
or yesterday's kids playing tag around the house?
Do you smell the rotting wood of the rickety frame
or the farmer's wife's newly baked bread?
Do you feel the house should be pulled down
or left for hay to be stacked inside
and sheltered by a corrugated roof
that is probably older than you or I?

The Ambrose Trust cottage (demolished in 2004)
was built in 1869 as the first post office and library
in Whitford, Auckland. Verandahs offered
protection from rain, wind and sun.

Right: The smallest post office in New Zealand was
at Wharerata, in the Gisborne region, in the 1920s.

Our tiny little post office
Was corrugated tin
Someone beat me to it
So I could not get in.

'The Diggers' joke' ~
Kiwi soldiers in World War I
make their mark of national identity.
Location uncertain, possibly France.
RSA COLLECTION, ALEXANDER TURNBULL LIBRARY G13585 1/2

'Betsy and friend':
Milking a house cow,
Stratford area, circa 1900.
JAMES MCALLISTER COLLECTION,
ALEXANDER TURNBULL LIBRARY G9611 1/1

Other places ~ other uses

Corrugated iron has the same advantages and disadvantages it did over a century ago and when an enterprising spirit is faced with a lack of cash or technical know-how, there is little wonder that its uses are sometimes extraordinary.

The idea of a corrugated coracle or canoe must have occurred to many young minds, but those of us who actually built one found by experience that the necessary stability was seriously lacking. One unusual use of corrugated iron came about because of its inherent strength in comparison to its weight. In 1915 Hugo Junkers, the German aeronautical engineer, patented and constructed the first all-metal aircraft using a steel-welded frame and corrugated iron. Instead of using wood and fabric he used the metal as 'stressed skin' to help distribute the stresses. His Junkers aircraft, nicknamed the Tin Donkey, gained respect for its innovation, and its successors became the most popular aircraft of the time. In the 1920s and '30s almost all of the world's airlines were using Junkers G24 aircraft that had three engines and carried nine passengers.

The corrugated way to fly! Junkers first used corrugated iron, Ford used corrugated duralumin.
Jürg Andermatt/Lufthansa Bordbuch

Car manufacturer Henry Ford built aircraft engines during World War I, and after producing his 10 millionth 'Tin Lizzie' car in 1924 he turned his attention to aircraft. Like Junkers, he was sold on the idea of metal aircraft and recognised that metal multi-engined monoplanes would be the aircraft of the future. In 1925 he bought the Stout Aircraft Company, which already built monoplanes, but clad them with corrugated Duralumin instead of steel as Junkers had done. (Duralumin is an aluminium alloy containing copper for strength.)

Ford's first plane, the Tri-motor 4AT, carried twelve passengers and used a corrugated skin, with the corrugations aligned to minimise drag. Ford's plane had great similarity to Junkers' designs, which led to a suit for patent violation. Ford went on not only to make planes but also to found his own airline, with the first modern airport in the United States at Dearborn, Michigan, the site of the present Ford museum.

Ford's Tri-motor was the plane which flew Admiral Byrd over the South Pole in 1929 and took Charles Lindbergh on America's first transcontinental passenger service. This plane was very successful and 195 were built and sold to airlines all around the world. Manufacture was discontinued in 1933 because of the downturn in sales during the economic depression.

The Tri-motor was affectionately known as the Tin Goose, because of its ungainly progress down the mile-long runway 'honking' as it went, or as the 'flying washboard' because of its corrugated construction.

Another almost unbelievable use of corrugated iron was the New Zealand army's Semple tank. This 'Dad's Army' apparition was born out of necessity during World War II because of the shortage of materials from overseas. A D8 bulldozer was armoured up with corrugated steel, supposedly to fend off the arrows of the enemy. It is believed that its most important function was to bolster the morale of people who were getting apprehensive about Japanese invasion. The Semple tank (nicknamed the 'Septic tank') was named after the colourful Labour leader Bob Semple, who in 1941 was minister both of Works and of National Service.

The New Zealand army's
'Semple' tank, a converted bulldozer.
NEW ZEALAND ARMY MUSEUM

Our Army isn't up to much
If we are really frank
How could you stop the enemy
With a corrugated tank?

The farmer's friend

Corrugated iron has been used in so many ways in the past that it has become a Kiwi icon, with a historic and aesthetic value we are emotionally attached to.

Housing is its biggest use, and not just for humans. Corrugated dog kennels, pig pens and goat houses abound throughout New Zealand. Farm sheds, shearing sheds, barns, stables, baches, verandahs, mountain huts, tree-huts, chook-houses and storage buildings are all part of the landscape.

Shearing shed, location and photographer unknown. Shorn sheep are about to jump through 'portholes' into counting-out pens. Woolsacks at the windows provide shade for the shearers.
Alexander Turnbull Library F23109 1/4

There was a tin shed in Kaitaia
Local farmers used to admire
What unsettled their nerves
Were the sinuous curves
All consumed by agricultural desire

Right: Haybarn near Pukerua Bay,
and below, near Ohakune.
JOCELYN CARLIN

Do you have nostalgic thoughts
Of when you were a kid?
Cos we had a big red shed
Before the Warehouse did.

Corrugated iron is not just a roofing material. It has been used for water tanks, fences, dunnies, shower linings, chimneys, barbecue plates, urinals, canoes, toboggans, haystack covers, grain silos … the list goes on.

Not only is it one of the original do-it-yourself materials but also one of the original recyclable materials. When repairs are done, the old stuff is carefully put away 'for a rainy day' under the house or at the back of the garage. The farming community builds simple, useful buildings in their own way: behind most farm sheds is a miscellaneous pile of stuff that you can be pretty certain contains a stack of old sheets of corrugate. Some farm buildings have been around since the colony was settled and today corrugated cladding is still the farmer's favourite.

Corrugated iron is a most suitable material for grain silos because it can be curved as well as corrugated. It withstands internal pressures from the weight of grain and resists the external compressive wind forces when it is empty. It is a pragmatic solution and an excellent technical one as well.

Grain silos were originally imported from the United States and Europe but local ingenuity soon extended the corrugated tank vertically to become a conspicuous part of the landscape. Dan Cosgrove in Timaru produced corrugated silos that have changed the skyline, particularly around the Canterbury plains.

One of Dan Cosgrove's characteristic feed silos, manufactured in Timaru.
DAN COSGROVE LTD

Bisley silos near Balclutha.

This ruminant is funny
He easily gets my vote
He's always up to something
Acting the giddy goat.

This corrugated shelter
Has not allowed for growth
Bo-peep's lamb now has a choice
Its head or bum ~ not both

This corrugated doghouse
Belongs to my dog Tim.
When I've been misbehaving
I have to share with him.

Tim's corrugated doghouse
Is not the best of homes
Because it isn't furnished
It only has bare bones.

This corrugated mailbox
Makes the townies snigger
But Farmer Jones has planned ahead
Cos his bills are getting bigger.

Water tanks

Galvanised corrugated tanks are as much part of the Australasian scene as the material itself. Although ideal for a roof, the galvanised material can be unsuitable for water storage because, being submerged, the necessary protective film does not always form on the zinc coating.

Most tanks are now fed from bores, wells or springs with water containing dissolved minerals that can attack galvanised coating. Tanks have to be replaced after five to ten years, which pleases the plumber because it provides him with a fill-in job, a wet-weather one if it's an inside tank. Tanks of 400 or 600 gallons were standard for outside, and 60 gallons for an attic. Years ago, galvanised corrugated tanks were often placed in the attic to feed the copper hot water cylinder, but when the exhaust pipe overflowed back into the tank, hot water containing copper salts greatly accelerated corrosion. A great trade was done curving, riveting and soldering tank after tank after tank.

The corrugated sheet was curved in a pyramid-rolling machine, as shown on page 34. The curve was rolled to the required radius by progressively adjusting the pressure on the top rolls.

Tips to make your galvanised corrugated iron tank last longer

- Each tank should have its own separate inlet and outlet. Don't connect them in series.
- Don't overflow one tank into the other.
- Don't use copper or brass fittings on your corrugated tank. Filling it from copper spouting or downpipes is a real no-no!
- Keep tree debris out of your tank ~ clean it out when you get the chance.
- Use damp-proof course to insulate the tank bottom from the timber bearers as they will be H3 treated, probably with copper preservative.
- Place your tank away from the full sun ~ heating the water accelerates corrosion.

- Don't let your tank fill to the brim for its first fill. Give it time to let the protective film build up gradually. There are proprietary materials available containing meta-phosphates that can help give a protective film.
- Inlet water should discharge directly into the water, not dribble down the inside of the tank.
- If the water is known to be corrosive then paint the inside of the tank, but only when it is new, using a high-build epoxy or other thick barrier coating.
- If the catchment roof is Colorsteel or aluminium/zinc (AZ) coated steel, tanks should not be used without first coating the inside.
- If your water is alkaline do not use an AZ-coated tank without a high-build coating.

COLIN MARTIN

Nissen and Quonset huts in many sizes and guises: Top, at Evans Bay; the blue shed is in Hastings; lower right at Manor Park.
MARILYN COLES

The tragedy of war
Of all our young men sent needlessly
Their sleeping hours in wet trenches
Or a tent
For some a better shelter though
All steel and corrugated
Called a Nissen or a Quonset Hut
Plus a lot of other names
The editor has cut

The Heine machine in the picture was a hand roller, and I know from personal experience after a day's work there was no need to visit the gym.

As an apprentice I was given a job as the 'dollyman'. For this 'inside job' I had to hold a steel bar called the dolly, shaped to follow the corrugation, adjacent to where a hole was punched through the sheet lap from the outside. A tinman's rivet was placed in the hole, the dolly placed behind the rivet head and the lucky one with the outside job would set the rivet with a hammer. It doesn't take much to imagine the din inside the tank. Sixty years ago there weren't such things as pop rivets or earmuffs. My mother used to wonder where all her cotton wool went!

Wartime necessities: Nissen and Quonset huts

During World War I the British Army needed buildings they could set up quickly and easily as temporary accommodation for men in the field. Captain Peter Nissen, a Canadian serving in the Royal Engineers in France, had an idea for the design of semicircular huts using corrugated iron. This idea was not original, as buildings had been made in this shape since 1840 and some were used in the Crimean war in 1853, but most army hut designs had been gabled, with walls and eaves. (The World War II New Zealand army four-man hut was like this, with a corrugated roof.)

The Brits took up Nissen's idea and he oversaw design and construction of a prototype. In 1916 the first order was placed for corrugated iron sheets with Braby & Co in England and over 100,000 huts were supplied to France and Belgium. After the war, the promoted Lieutenant-Colonel Nissen was awarded the Distinguished Service Order and offered £500 for his invention. He considered the offer inadequate, and eventually accepted £10,000.

Some of the original huts had bent timber frames, which were later replaced with steel tee frames 16 feet wide by 27 feet long. Building a Nissen hut normally took six men four hours, but the record is just under 90 minutes. The original internal timber linings were changed to vertical corrugated iron after troops used them for firewood!

Nissen huts were used extensively by the army and air force in World War II, and in the Falklands war in 1982. They can still be seen today on defence bases around the world and are remembered well by those who had to live in them.

With the threat of war in 1941 the US Navy also needed a cheap, lightweight, portable structure that could be built by unskilled personnel. The George A Fuller Construction Co of New York was given two months to come up with a prototype for a version of the Nissen hut and a production facility was quickly set up near Quonset, Rhode Island.

The Quonset was similar to the Nissen hut, with a row of semicircular steel ribs covered with corrugated sheets. A little wider at 20 feet and longer at 48 feet, it had a steel-frame foundation with a plywood floor. It could be extended to any length and came in many versions. Over 170,000 were produced during World War II and sold afterwards for about US $1000 each for housing, business, storage and even as churches. Many can still be seen throughout the US and the Pacific.

Anderson shelters, the backyard air-raid shelters of World War II, were another common use of corrugated iron during the war.

Chris Seymour shearing on the Chatham Islands.
Jocelyn Carlin

Sweet scent of warm lanoline
Dripping sweat of the burly contractor
Incessant whir of cutting blades
Scampering scud of escaping sheep
Unfrightened eye of the knowing victim
The farmer's smile at the growing pile
Constant sweep of the wooden floor
Mounting excitement of the rising tally
Increasing weariness of the day's end
Anticipated taste of the first beer
Radiating heat of the wrinkly tin
Unique world of the shearing shed.

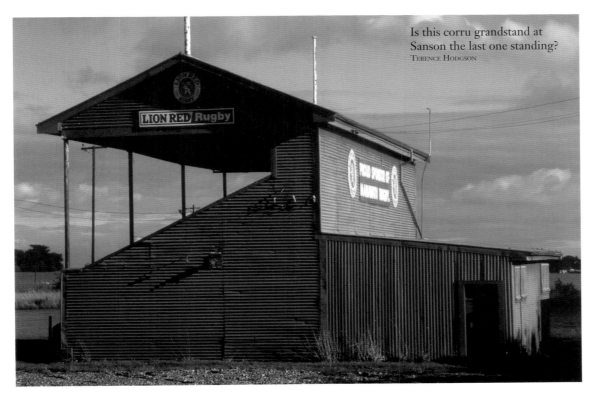

Is this corru grandstand at Sanson the last one standing?
Terence Hodgson

When you're done and you're had it
And left with no breath
Like this old tank
Is there life after death?

Our corrugated bus shed
Makes us justifiably proud
It really was made for one though
So two is a cosy crowd

Bus shelters, wood shelters, dunnies ~
all are useful members of society.

A two-person long-drop with a view on Waiheke Island.
COLIN MARTIN

When there's a big job to be done
Two heads are better than one
But those of Caucasian persuasion
Regard this solemn occasion,
As a private and solitary one.

The long-drop, or thunderbox, is well known to many New Zealanders but the very young may now miss out on that experience.

You may think it somewhat strange
Or maybe even funny
How sadly I mourn the passing
Of our corrugated dunny.

I could go and hide there
When mum was in a mood
I found some peace and quiet there ~
Until I needed food

I used to leave the door open
When the sky was full of stars
And gaze up at the Milky Way
To find that red one ~ Mars.

I used to meet my friends there
I called them Daphne and Chloe
They were long-legged spiders
Beside my weta Joey.

Sometimes I had a crisis
And nearly got caught short
I was relieved and grateful
If the daily paper had been bought.

Quite often it was crummy
And far from automatic
But our 'wrinkly tin' old dunny
Was always so pragmatic

I miss my daily exercise
The dash down the garden path
Now that the flushing loo
Sits by the basin and bath

We are all so pure and clean now
On sanitation bent
I couldn't even build one now
I'd never get resource consent.

JEAN CASH

The question for me
About this vis-à-vis
Is its gender inflexible
Asexual or bisexual?

Below: A view of the wide Pacific from this throne on the Chatham Islands.
JOCELYN CARLIN

The backdrop is so superb
It engenders my belief,
The front-drop is superb as well
It engenders my relief.

French Ridge Hut, Mt Aspiring National Park.
SHAUN BARNETT/BLACK ROBIN PHOTOGRAPHY

Bruce Postill at
Makakoere Hut,
Te Urewera
National Park.
Shaun Barnett/
Black Robin Photography

The end of a hard day's slog: the welcome glimpse of the corrugated hut, an unlocked door,
neatly stacked firewood, smoky tea from the steaming billy, the bullet hail on the tin roof,
the misty sunrise, the scent of the New Zealand bush … the end of a hard day's slog.

Opposite page, left: Back Ridge Hut, Kaweka Forest Park; Trident Hut, Kahurangi National Park on the right.
SHAUN BARNETT/BLACK ROBIN PHOTOGRAPHY

This page: Forks Hut, Ruahine Forest Park. Despite not performing so well as a thermal insulation, corrugated iron can be easily transported into remote places and the huts it clads are always a welcome sight for trampers.
SHAUN BARNETT/HEDGEHOG HOUSE

The man from the Council
Says "in our District Scheme
Your hut is not at all PC,
I want it painted green"

Above: Wharf building in
New Plymouth;
Above right: Farm shed
in the Nelson Bays,
behind a lichen-covered
totara fence;
Right: Fertiliser works,
Te Kuiti.

Big and small,
short and tall,
I can cope
With them all.

Left: Boatsheds high and dry at low tide.
Viv Adamson

Below: Auckland's Ngapipi Road boaties, gone fishin'.

Ann McNaught

Another recreational use of corrugated iron is scattered near beaches around New Zealand. The Titahi Bay corrugated iron boatsheds (left), although often threatened by extinction via the bureaucracy, have survived and remain a Bay icon.

Corrugated iron gives impressive bracing, as witnessed on 10 April 1968 ~ Wahine Day. Cyclone Giselle hit Titahi Bay that morning with a fury never to be forgotten. My home overlooked these boatsheds; three were uplifted from their sandy foundations and hurled into our house, causing major damage.

While I was trying to save my house and the next-door neighbour's from destruction I saw a bizarre sight. Traumatised and beginning to suffer from hypothermia, I saw my own boatshed lift off like a helicopter and fly over my head, still in its boatshed shape. My only reaction was "Oh, there goes another boatshed." The walls opened out but the corrugated iron trussed roof kept rising and disappeared into the murk. Neither it, nor the clinker-built boat next door, were ever seen again.

I loved to get me all togged up
To go to hear the band
I loved their shiny instruments
Their uniforms were grand

I loved to hear my Uncle Ken
He played a big trombone
I don't think that my aunty did
When he practised it at home

I loved the big conductor man
With that stick he used to throw
And thought that maybe someday soon
That I could have a go

I loved the bandstand in the park
I hope it's not a sin
But I think that I first fell in love
With its roof of wrinkly tin

I loved that huge brass curly-cue
That made a sound like thunder
I always knew when I grew up
I'd play on our rotunda

In days gone by Sunday was a day of rest, visiting
and walking ~ sometimes to enjoy a brass band
playing at the rotunda in the village, the seaside
or the gardens. Its hexagonal or octagonal roof
suited curved corrugated iron. Below: Inglewood.
ANNIE MCNAUGHT

JOHN SOUTHALL

Above: This Cambridge attraction may be the only one of its kind in New Zealand. It was built in 1910
with a dressing room, tea room, and band rotunda on top. The octagonal pavilion, 18 feet in diameter, is
built of heart kauri and totara with ornamental cast-iron friezes, brackets and balustrade. The lead floor in
the upper storey has sufficient camber to let the rain run off.

Hundreds of people attended the opening in 1910 where the member of parliament Mr WH Herries
did the honours. The band played, there were speeches, the ladies' committee put on afternoon tea and
the young men entertained with a game of hockey.

In 1921 the pavilion was moved from Bracken Street to Leamington Domain, towed by a traction
engine. Shelter and ornamental trees were planted, football grounds were laid out and tennis courts made.

In 1983 council wanted to demolish the bottom storey and re-site the rotunda in Victoria Square. The
Cambridge Historical Society appealed through the *Top Half* TV programme to preserve the rotunda.
A deluge of letters was sent to the Council and the rotunda was saved and renovated.

Making it here

In an advertisement in *Wise's Directory* of 1875/76, R & T Haworth ~ wholesale and retail iron merchants from Princes Street, Dunedin ~ made claim to be manufacturers of corrugated iron. That claim extended to sheet copper and block tin as well, so it is likely that these materials were in fact not made by Haworths, but imported and sold by them.

It is thought that the first corrugated iron actually produced in New Zealand was made in 1886 in Auckland by Samuel Parker, who imported steel sheets to galvanise and corrugate in his Southern Cross Galvanised Iron Manufacturing Co at Mechanics Bay. Parker's iron had the support of the government, which specified New Zealand-made product in preference to the imported stuff. This may have been the first 'Made in New Zealand' preferential government support for local industry, a policy that was to continue until the 1970s.

Corrugated iron was a steadily growing import from the 1860s to the 1960s, except during world wars. Because of British defence usage, shipments reduced from 20,000 tons in 1936 and 1937 to 13,000 tons in 1938 and 16,000 in 1939. Stocks normally carried amounted to some 5000 tons, or three months' supply. At the outbreak of war in 1939, stocks of corrugated iron were low and the upsurge of defence construction work led to shortages. A reserve stock of 2000 tons (valued at £60,000) had been set aside prior to 1939 by the Public Works Department for defence buildings, but this was only three-quarters of the estimated requirement for emergency buildings alone and just five weeks' supply of corrugated iron for the whole country.

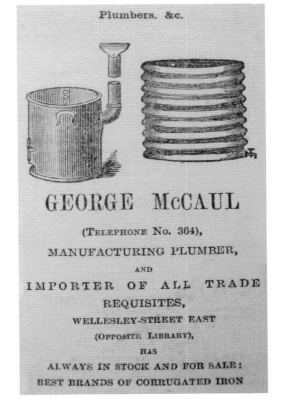

Plumbers, &c.

GEORGE McCAUL

(TELEPHONE No. 364),

MANUFACTURING PLUMBER,

AND

IMPORTER OF ALL TRADE REQUISITES,

WELLESLEY-STREET EAST
(OPPOSITE LIBRARY),

HAS

ALWAYS IN STOCK AND FOR SALE:
BEST BRANDS OF CORRUGATED IRON

R. & T. HAWORTH,
Wholesale & Retail Iron Merchants,
AND MANUFACTURERS OF
PLAIN CORRUGATED IRON, ZINC, BLOCK TIN, & SHEET COPPER,
GALVANIZED IRON AND SPOUTING,
Ridge Cap, Black Corrugated Iron, Piping Heads, Shoes, Brackets, &c. Also the newly-invented Galvanized Iron Fluming for Water Races and Mining Purposes.
PRINCES STREET, DUNEDIN.

In 1940 imports totalled 9000 tons, under half that imported in 1937, and for the rest of the war they averaged a little over 2000 tons a year. The scarcity of corrugated iron was a principal cause of restrictions on private building throughout the war. These same restrictions were imposed on the use of steel until 1954, during which time demand exceeded supply fourfold.

Because new corrugated iron for building was prohibited and galvanised flat iron could only be used for window and door flashings, malthoid-covered roofs and wooden gutters became a sign of wartime shortages. Government restrictions stopped the use of new corrugated iron without a permit, but it was surprising how many new corrugated roofs ended up painted to resemble second-hand iron that did not face the same restrictions.

The worldwide shortage of steel, and government controls on the importation of corrugated iron, meant that alternatives had to be found. Cheap corrugated aluminium was imported from Japan, made out of scrap from melted-down Zero fighter planes or any other aluminium that could be found. The alloy content was not well controlled and because it contained copper, and the gauge material was a thin 24g SWG .022 inch (.56mm), it often pitted and corroded to perforation within a few years, particularly near the sea. It was used for spouting and downpipes because it could not be soldered. I became a part-time welding instructor at the Acetone Illuminating & Welding Company in Wellington. For 24g aluminium we used a brazing technique, which was tricky to say the least.

Another reason corrugated aluminium failed was the old lead-head nail used to fix it, which caused deterioration in high corrosion areas. In contrast, higher quality, heavier gauge manganese alloy aluminium subsequently imported from Alcan (Canada) and Alcoa (USA) has performed well in such areas. Post-war years also saw corrugated asbestos sheeting imported because of the worldwide steel shortage.

New Zealand importers represented individual British steel mills during the pre- and post-war periods until the nationalisation of the UK steel industry in 1948. Gollins, Nathans, Richard Thomas Baldwin, AM Satterthwaite and John Burns all imported from the UK and John Lysaght imported from its factory in Australia. Together, these companies formed the tight-knit Galvanised Sheet Guild, a group of merchant distributors holding a monopoly on galvanised steel entering New Zealand as a result of the import control system.

Steel was sourced from wherever it could be found. Corrugated and flat galvanised steel came from United States Steel, Kawasaki and Yawata in Japan and Iscor from South Africa, in addition to traditional sources.

Archaeologists at Te Wairoa unearthed these tanks buried, along with the Pink & White Terraces, in the Tarawera eruption of 1886.
Hugh Patterson/WriteWords Ltd

Factories small and large

Just after World War II John Lysaght installed a barrel corrugator in a building on Thorndon Quay, Wellington and made stock lengths of corrugated roofing with sheet imported from their rolling mills in Australia. The din of this machine could be heard streets away and neighbours were pleased when it was finally relegated to be a boat mooring at Evans Bay.

The pioneer of roll-forming corrugated iron in New Zealand was Ness Irwin. He built his own machine around 1962 and his Mt Roskill factory began to produce two widths of corrugation profile marketed as Longrun. During its first four years NS Irwin Ltd had little local competition, but the advantage of cut-to-length roof cladding was soon recognised.

In 1966 Hayes Engineering in Rotorua made and sold eight machines which all started rolling corrugated iron in New Zealand. Norsteel Roll Formed Products (later to become Fletchers) also started manufacturing at this time.

John Lysaght Australia were selling approximately 15% of their galvanised production here and through the import licensing system had established a 70% market share. When they heard that New Zealand Steel proposed to build a galvanising line and corrugator in Auckland they put forward a proposal to do the same, using second-hand plant from Australia. Their proposal did not eventuate but New Zealand Steel recognised Lysaght's marketing position by engaging them as a mill agent, which gave them purchasing rights to 70% of NZ Steel's output. The balance was split among the other traditional importers, Richard Thomas Baldwin, Satterthwaites and Nathans, in direct proportion to their import licensing history.

Construction delays at New Zealand Steel led to some corrugated iron toll-rolling (labour only) contracts being negotiated with Irwins in Auckland and Dimond Industries in Wellington to manufacture stock lengths before NZ Steel started making it themselves. Steel merchants became the stockists of standard lengths of corrugated sheeting and large quantities went into the rural and domestic markets.

Another local pioneer was Owen Marshall of Invercargill, who also made his own machine and began to produce an aptly-named Pioneer brand corrugate. My own company built a roll-forming machine in 1963 that rolled a secret-fix profile called Tomet. This profile is clip-fixed, not nail-fixed, and was the first such profile to be made here.

In 1968 New Zealand Steel purchased a large roll-forming machine from the Yoder Mills in the US to roll corrugated steel in lengths from 5 to 12 feet in one-foot increments. This 12-stand roll-former had three and a half inch diameter shafts and was installed alongside the

Auckland's corrugated iron pioneer Ness Irwin beside the machine he built to produce New Zealand's first long-run roofing steel.

galvanising line at Glenbrook. This machine was state-of-the-art at the time. The process was automated, having a 60-ton flying shear and a magnetic pick-up roller table which accelerated the cut sheet out of the way of the next one being rolled. It also had a 'walking table' that moved the stacked sheets away for packing. Though designed to roll from 32 gauge to 16 gauge material, the big Yoder always seemed to be an overkill just for corrugating steel. The sheets were cut on the run and the machine sequencing was controlled by integrated circuits that were made in the UK and were very new at the time.

This machine was the baby of New Zealand Steel's Dave Collins: "We didn't have any training in integrated circuitry and it was a difficult machine to keep operational. Sometimes we worked around the clock ~ on salary, without pay. Calls were so frequent that I kept a set of drawings under my bed at home and often solved the problem over the phone!"

The machine could roll 76 metres of corrugate per minute and produce 10 tons an hour. Production began in 1969 and some 30,000 tons were made each year, with about 80% destined for local markets through the mill agents and sold under the brand Glenzinc.

Corrugated iron was also produced for the US market, which required different profiles from ours, a 2¾ inch and a 2½ inch pitch rather than the standard 3 inch.

Hayes days

From 1966 on, small roll-forming machines proliferated all around the country, most manufactured by Hayes Engineering in Rotorua. Hayes began making a seven-stand machine with 'across the board' tooling, selling for around £12,000, although these small seven-roll machines could form only 24 and 26 gauge soft steel.

Hayes' machines cost a tenth of New Zealand Steel's big Yoder, and for this modest investment small manufacturers could make and sell roofing direct, cutting out all the middlemen. Merchant margins at the time were as high as 40%, particularly in the South Island, but time and competition saw the price of corrugated iron drastically reduced.

Tom Hayes' company exported roll-forming machines all around the world, but as they became more sophisticated they also became more expensive. The use of high-strength steel required a stronger machine with more forming stands, so after 1968 the original seven were upped to nine, then 11, and eventually 15. 'Arrow-head' forming was adopted in 1980 (so named because it resembles an arrowhead when viewed from the front).

In eight years Hayes sold 23 machines in New Zealand and a total of 56 in 14 years.

New Zealand Steel's
Yoder roll-former.
NEW ZEALAND STEEL

NZ METAL ROOFING MANUFACTURERS INC.

Tom Hayes MNZM at home in Rotorua.
DEBBIE AITCHISON

Manufacturers worldwide cannot believe that New Zealand has so many corrugating machines … Never have so many machines been sold to so many for a market where the people are so few! (with apologies to Winston Churchill.)

Most of the early manufacturers who purchased Hayes machines (plus those that made their own) formed the Corrugated Steel Manufacturers Association in 1966. Their executive consisted of Ted Howarth (Dimond Industries Ltd, Wellington) chairman, Gerald Burton (LG Pope Ltd, Stratford), Alan Brockelsby (AC Brockelsby & Co Ltd, Wellington), Bruce Columbus (Oakleys Ltd, Christchurch), Dan Cosgrove (Dan Cosgrove Ltd, Timaru), Jim Gardner (HR Gardner & Sons Ltd, Dunedin), and Ness Irwin (NS Irwin Ltd, Auckland). This association later joined with the Profile Cladding Manufacturers Association and the New Zealand Spouting & Downpipe Association to form the New Zealand Metal Roofing Manufacturers Association. Most of the original companies are still members of the Metal Roofing Manufacturers.

New Zealand Steel sold freight-paid steel anywhere in New Zealand and their Yoder met all New Zealand's needs, but their market dried up within a few years because local machines were supplying their own areas. This major development occurred for three reasons:

- Merchants stocked only standard length sheets, whereas local machines could supply sheets cut to any length and avoid end laps.
- Manufacturers could sell direct and deliver to the site, limited only by transport restrictions.
- The government at that time provided protection for New Zealand Railways: you needed a permit to transport your own production more than 30 miles from your factory, and all other material had to go by rail. This was the Muldoon era of controls.

Jeff Ward of Ward Engineering in Christchurch also made corrugating machines but his, at £30,000 or so, were more expensive than a Hayes machine. Dimond Industries bought five 'raft' machines which were more sophisticated and could roll other profiles. Ward also manufactured the flying cut-off for New Zealand Steel's corrugator, made to Yoder's design.

Norsteel Roll Formed Products bought one of Ward's first roll-formers and began to make an impression on the corrugated iron market. This machine was eventually bought by Fletchers (later to become Fletcher Brownbuilt), who with Dimond Industries became a dominant player in the roofing market in the 1970s and '80s.

Hayes Engineering also sold corrugators into Australia and made an impact on the monopoly held by John Lysaght in manufacturing corrugated iron. Tom Hayes says:

In 1970 I received a visit from two senior Lysaght personnel looking for the person who had affected their exports to New Zealand. By that date we had about fifteen corrugating machines producing in New Zealand. Both the visitors wore black suits and arrived in a black car, while I wore only overalls because I was working in the factory.

They wanted to look at a machine, and I took them into the workshop as we had one almost finished. After inspection I was advised that had there been any patents on corrugated iron I would be slaughtered, but luckily for me there were none.

The senior gentleman then offered his hand and congratulated me for producing such a simple and small machine that produced good quality corrugated roofing cut-to-length with a flying shear. I was very happy to shake their hands, as it was much better than looking down the barrel of a .44!

We really knew little about roll-form tooling design because there was nothing published about it ~ roll-forming was not a big industry at that time. And our customers knew as little as we did. When a problem occurred anywhere in New Zealand it was out to the Rotorua aerodrome and off we would race to Christchurch or Nelson or New Plymouth or wherever, to check and overcome the problem. The only way we could learn about and improve our machines was to inspect and check anything that didn't appear to be correct.

We kept a big black book that we called the Design Bible. In this we recorded our mistakes and errors and what was done to correct them, in the hope that they were not repeated.

New Zealand Steel stopped making corrugated steel for the local market around 1980, and in 1982 they employed me as a development engineer to design a trapezoidal profile for the roof and walls of new buildings at the mill. The profile was to be produced on the big Yoder and was named Steelspan.

I was not welcome at the Glenbrook Mill. Strong union demarcation was prevalent at this time so that if you were not a member of the right union, using a spanner was *verboten*. After narrowly avoiding a full-scale strike at the mill, the old Yoder corrugator machine at Glenbrook was decommissioned in 1982 and shifted to Steltech Developments at Takanini, Manukau.

Steltech was set up by New Zealand Steel as a subsidiary specifically for product development.

HAYES INTERNATIONAL (WWW.HAYESINT.COM)

Tom Hayes' roll-formers, showing different tool design methods: above is 'across the board' and on the opposite page is 'arrowhead'.

The Yoder was retooled and fitted with new electronics. Once the New Zealand Steel buildings had been roofed and clad with Steelspan, the profile was sold on the open market.

After the government withdrew tax incentives for research and development the old Yoder corrugator was eventually sold to Malaysia. Thus ended New Zealand Steel's foray into the corrugated roofing market.

While at Steltech I noticed discrepancies among the corrugated steel from many manufacturers and tested each of their profiles to see if they met the industry standard. One roll-former even had wooden rollers, but made quite a good profile in soft material (G250Mpa).

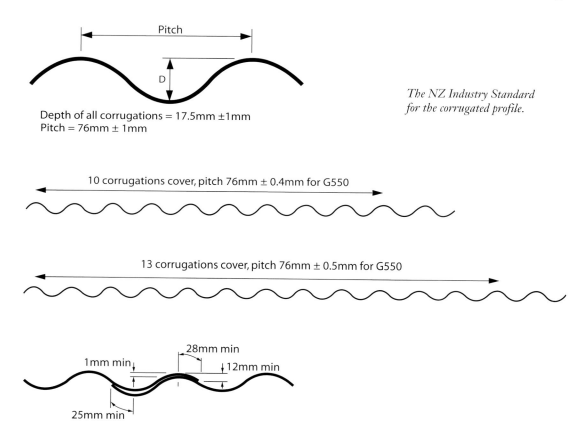

The NZ Industry Standard for the corrugated profile.

In the 1960s and '70s our standard for corrugated iron was NZS1343:1960, which was a copy of the old British standard in which each corrugation was three-quarters of an inch deep and three inches in pitch. NZS3403:1978 was a metric conversion of the old standard. In spite of lobbying, Standards New Zealand did not take into account that by this time most corrugated iron made here was high-strength steel and did not meet these dimensions. Continued pressure was placed on the authorities to change the standard, and it was finally withdrawn in 2004. The industry standard has been followed for the last 30 years and is shown in the drawings opposite. The Standard 17.5mm depth ± 1mm is higher than that now required in Australia.

Advances in metallurgy in the 20th century enabled the manufacture of steel with a greater range of mechanical properties, and the use of a greater amount of scrap metal. From the 1970s most corrugated iron made in New Zealand used high-strength steel coil with about twice the strength of previous softer steels.

The high strength steel produced by cold rolling meant that most of the early New Zealand machines that had been roll-forming the softer material had to be upgraded. Needless to say Tom Hayes took full advantage of this opportunity.

There are several ways to roll-form corrugated iron. Tom Hayes' first machines used 'across the board' tooling where all the following rolls are the same shape but each set is lowered more than the one before it. This tool design is called *air-forming* because the rollers are not shaped exactly to the profile. It can lead to splitting in the middle of the sheet, and the corrugations are not necessarily the same depth across the sheet.

A better way to corrugate iron is to use *arrow-head forming* where each corrugation, or pair of corrugations, is completed before the next one is started.

HAYES INTERNATIONAL (WWW.HAYESINT.COM)

Tom Hayes, the corrugator from Rotorua
Loved a real challenge, that's for sure
But success ain't all that it seems,
Cos he sold so many machines
That his customers got fewer and fewer.

A selection of Australian brands.

Detail of Adelaide Superdrome,
designed by Carlo Gnezda.
PETER HYATT, *INNOVATIONS IN STEEL*
(INTERNATIONAL IRON & STEEL INSTITUTE)

Across the ditch

In 1918 John Lysaght (Australia) Pty was established to import galvanised steel from Lysaght's Bristol factory, which was then sold under the Orb brand. Two years later John Lysaght established a mill in Newcastle, Australia, to roll and galvanise sheet using steel from the recently completed Broken Hill Proprietary (BHP) plant nearby. The paths of John Lysaght and BHP in Australia were intertwined from that time until their sale in 2003.

In 1936 Lysaght started a new works at Port Kembla, NSW, and within three years these two plants were producing all the galvanised iron Australia needed, and exporting to New Zealand and the Pacific. They set up a continuous galvanising line at Port Kembla in 1955 and another at Newcastle in 1961.

In 1970 BHP became joint owners of Lysaghts with Guest, Keen and Nettlefold, who still owned John Lysaght in the UK. When BHP acquired GKN's shares in 1979, John Lysaght (Australia) Pty became a wholly owned subsidiary of BHP.

In 1972 a new 'cold strip' plant opened at Western Port, Victoria, which included a five-stand cold strip mill and a 1500mm-wide galvanising and strip painting line. In 1976 the company introduced the aluminium/zinc alloy Zincalume to replace the traditional zinc used for galvanising. After the BHP reorganisation in 1985, John Lysaght (Australia) became its Coated Products Division. In 2001 BHP merged with the huge British resources group Billiton, but it became a separate company in 2003 and was listed on the stock exchange under the name BlueScope Steel.

Of course some Australians still think they own corrugated iron ~ like pavlova, Russell Crowe and Phar Lap.

Left: Tanks feature in buildings by Australia's
renowned corrugated iron architect, Glenn Murcutt …
COURTESY PHILIP DREW; REINER BLUNCK, *INNOVATIONS IN STEEL* (INTERNATIONAL IRON & STEEL INSTITUTE)

I bought a little water tank
Of corrugated iron
Because there were just two of us
It suited us just fine

But then our family grew and grew
And two plus two was four
It soon was quite obvious
We were in need of more

So I bought another water tank
Of corrugated iron
Because there were just four of us
It suited us just fine

But then our family grew and grew
And two plus four was six
Running out of drinking water
Put us in a fix

So I bought another water tank
Of corrugated iron
Because there were just six of us
It suited us just fine

But then our family grew and grew
And two plus six was eight
This was now a crisis time
My wife was in a state.

She cried out loud ~ "Enuf … Enuf,"
(I owe her many thanks)
"We do not have the #%$@&# room
For any more water tanks."*

… and in the Kiwi bach.
PAUL THOMPSON, ALEXANDER TURNBULL
LIBRARY PA12 1336 09

Taranaki ironsands. The transformation of ironsand to corrugated iron is a remarkable and relatively unknown story.

From sand to steel

During his first voyage to New Zealand in 1769 Captain Cook noted large dune deposits of ironsands at Waikato North Head on the west coast of the North Island.

An early settler, John Perry, saw the abundance of black sand beneath his feet on arrival in New Plymouth and said, "I was astounded to see wealth spread out like a carpet." He tried to interest the New Zealand Company in this resource. Frederick Carrington, the New Zealand Company's surveyor for Taranaki, was so excited about the heavy black sand running through his hands in 1842 that he sent samples to England, Europe and elsewhere.

His dream was to make New Zealand into 'steel country' like England. The trials were not successful because of the presence of titanium in the ironsands, but local and central governments shared Carrington's vision. In 1857, 1873 and 1914 they offered monetary incentives for anyone able to develop this abundant resource. In 1857 the Taranaki provincial government offered £1000 for the first 100 tons of saleable iron. Although the New Zealand government upped this to £5000, they never had to pay out.

Several major companies attempted to take up these offers. In 1869 the Pioneer Steel Works tried at New Plymouth; followed by the New Zealand Titanic Iron & Steel Company at Te Henui beach, New Plymouth in 1873; and ten years later the NZ Iron & Steel Company at Onehunga. These and other small companies all failed to smelt the ironsands and the subsequent bankruptcies and financial losses cooled everyone's enthusiasm.

After the Iron and Steel Industries Act was passed in 1914 the NZ Iron Ore Smelting & Manufacturing Company at New Plymouth experimented using a blast furnace and did produce five tons of pig iron per day. They failed in the end because of the titanium carbide build-up in the furnace. In 1921 the Darlington Steel Works succeeded in making one ton of pig iron from twenty tons of ironsand shipped to England, but the process was not considered viable.

Because private enterprise had failed, the Labour government took matters into its own hands in 1937. It set up an Iron and Steel Commission to own a steelworks, without actually knowing how to smelt the ironsands economically.

"I was astounded to see wealth spread out like a carpet."

~ JOHN PERRY, ON ARRIVAL IN NEW PLYMOUTH

Analysing Taranaki ironsand in the 1950s.

After World War II, awareness grew that we were vulnerable as an economy based almost solely on grass. Both political parties wanted to see an iron and steel industry established, but by very different means. Labour wanted a nationalised industry but lost the election in 1949 and had to wait until they became the government again in 1957. The National government dismantled the Iron and Steel Department and repealed the Iron and Steel Act, believing that private enterprise, not the state, should develop the industry.

During that time many investigations were carried out by both government and private companies and in 1953 Fletchers sent samples of ironsand to Krupps in Germany for smelting trials. They made one big mistake. The sand was shipped out in honey tins and the labels proved too much of a temptation ~ the samples never arrived!

In 1955 Fletcher Holdings engaged Henry J Kaiser ~ of World War II Liberty Ship fame in the US ~ to assess the feasibility of an electric furnace at Taharoa, close to large deposits of ironsands. Again nothing eventuated, due to political factionalism and Fletchers' rivalry with the government-backed New Zealand Development Corporation.

Originally it was intended that to meet most of the country's flat steel requirements, New Zealand Steel would expand into a fully integrated industry and that scrap steelmaking and an eventual ironsand operation would merge.

Wellington bureaucrats were suspicious of overseas interests and even in government circles there was apprehension about Fletchers' dominance over New Zealand industry.

In 1958 the government decided that scrap-mill and ironsand steelmaking would be separate operations. Approval was given to Fletcher Holdings and Industrial Metals to make steel from scrap and eventually Stewart & Lloyds, GKN and RC McDonald became shareholders. The new company, Pacific Steel, started in 1962 and still operates an electric-arc furnace to melt iron and steel scrap, producing over 80% of our steel bar, rod and reinforcing requirements. It is now a member of the Fletcher Building Group.

In the 1950s our expanding economy led to increased demand for steel and renewed interest in making it from ironsand. Meanwhile, overseas, pilot scale pre-reduction and direct reduction processes were developing. Exploratory talks were held with Krupps of Germany and other steel mills, but little progress was made. We were spending more than we earned and the government needed rapid industrialisation to balance its budget and escape dependence on agricultural exports. The Labour Party won the 1957 election but lost again in 1960 ~ political instability and inflation all had an overlapping effect on the emerging iron and steel industry.

The late 1950s and '60s saw long and sometimes acrimonious dealings between government, Fletchers and New Zealand Steel over the allocation of scrap and the integration of the two mills ~ one using scrap and the other using ironsand.

The Iron and Steel Industry Act was passed again in 1959, vesting rights to the ironsands in the Crown. Once again an ironsand industry was on the agenda and the government was determined to proceed (Bill Sutch, head of the Industries and Commerce Department, in particular). The New Zealand Steel Investigating Co was set up, with Woolf Fisher as chairman, to determine the technical and economic feasibility of making steel from our ironsands and coal. They started a two-year research programme with the help of the US Battelle Memorial Institute of Columbus, Ohio, a metallurgical research foundation, and appointed a UK company, McLellan & Atkins, to prepare a feasibility study. The company's first job was to see how much ironsand there was ~ although the beaches were black from Wanganui to Kaipara, some of the sand was only windblown. They found extensive deposits of sand (titanomagnetite) which had blown out of ancient volcanos in Taranaki.

The Steel Investigating Co was assisted by the Department of Scientific and Industrial Research (DSIR) and other government departments to source the coal, limestone and water also needed to make steel.

Over 150,000,000 tons of ironsand were found at Waikato North Head, containing over 55% iron, and another 172,000,000 tons at Taharoa, south of Kawhia, a less accessible area.

The company was asked to find a possible site for the steel mill, and everything pointed to South Auckland. Glenbrook, 65km south of Auckland, was a good choice because it was close to rail, ironsand at Waikato North Head, the Waikato river, coal, and to nearly half of the market. Waikato coal reserves of 25 million tons were estimated to be sufficient for 50 years of production.

At this stage, of course, they had yet to discover an economic way to smelt the sand ~ the one thing that had eluded everybody.

The investigating company rejected the blast furnace option and in 1964 a direct reduction process called Stelco-Lurgi was adopted for further trials. Two hundred tons of ironsand were shipped off to the Lurgi plant in Frankfurt together with 135 tons of Waikato coal and four tons of limestone. The smelted product in pellet form was then shipped to the British Iron & Steel Research Association at Sheffield, and some went to Stelco at Edmonton, Canada to be melted in their electric-arc furnaces.

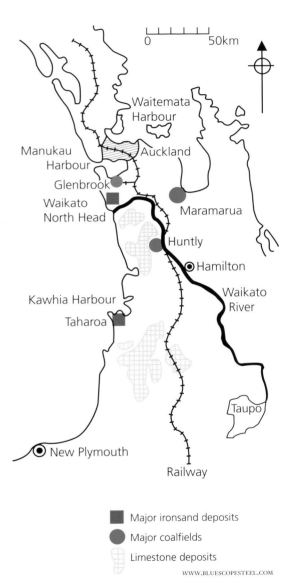

WWW.BLUESCOPESTEEL.COM

Ironsand on the west coast of the North Island, being fed onto a conveyor before it is transported in a slurry pipeline to the steel mill.

Based on the success of these trials New Zealand Steel was incorporated in 1965, and in 1967 they let contracts for a Stelco-Lurgi kiln, electric furnaces and a billet continuous casting machine. The original float of New Zealand Steel shares, although underwritten by the government, did not excite the sharemarket. The company ended up with about 50% ownership and had to front up with further funds by way of preference shares, although they were sold later to the public at considerable profit.

To provide cashflow for the large expansion it was decided that the downstream finished products would be made first from imported coil, which would be replaced with indigenous material later. The first development, including the galvanising plant, would begin ~ and this was a crucial decision.

British consultants were amazed at the huge per capita use of galvanised iron here, which was due to the popularity of corrugated iron. The ironsand project might not have survived without the sale of corrugate made by New Zealand Steel.

Meanwhile the arguments between Pacific Steel and New Zealand Steel came to a head when the latter announced plans to install a rod mill at Glenbrook. This controversy was finally resolved in 1965 when, in return for dropping the rod mill proposal, New Zealand Steel took a 42% shareholding in Pacific Steel.

Stage 1 construction started on the Glenbrook mill in 1966, and in 1968 the first commercial operations began producing corrugated and flat galvanised iron from imported Japanese coil for the domestic and Pacific Island markets.

The iron and steel plants were finally commissioned in 1970, but the Stelco-Lurgi plant did not scale up from the pilot plant as expected. This process, which required the sand to be ground down to fine particles and made into pellets, caused many headaches ~ but the problems were just beginning. As the pellets moved down the kiln they crumbled into powder and either stuck to the walls as part iron/coal build-up, or were blown out of the kiln by the waste gas and scattered over the countryside. This upset environmentalists, and kiwifruit farmers who did not appreciate this strange dust arriving on their property with the wind.

The birth ~ always an exhilarating time.
NEW ZEALAND STEEL

Men of steel:
Nigel Evans ...

Peter Bates

Rick Cooper

Ultimately, against the advice of foreign experts, pelletising was abandoned and unground ironsand concentrate was fed to the kiln. The new process evolved in incremental changes, including pre-heating the ore, which greatly increased the kiln capacity. These changes saved many steps, reduced costs and virtually eliminated the environmental problems.

Credit must be given to the resourcefulness of the 'young guns': Peter Bates, Nigel Evans, and Rick Cooper. Together with those on the mill floor and others they persevered during these early and difficult days and produced the first 'good stuff' in 1972.

From 1974 a New Zealand Steel programme known as 'backward integration' was planned to expand steelmaking fivefold and to include continuous slab-casting facilities and the installation of hot and cold strip mills. The government was involved because concessional rates had to be negotiated for government-supplied coal and electricity. Politicians, through Department of Industries and Commerce bureaucrats, had a heavy hand in what was to be done.

Although it had been approved, the government procrastinated on giving the go-ahead for this expansion.

With an election looming in 1981, Prime Minister Robert Muldoon was relying on his Think Big policies as a major plank of his economic strategy. He had lined up two projects: an aluminium smelter at Aramoana to be built by Fletchers in association with the big French company Pechiney, and a synthetic gasoline plant at Motunui with Mobil.

Just before the election both propositions fell flat. With almost indecent haste the Stage 2 planned expansion was suddenly given the green light, even though the project had long been planned and not a part of the Think Big strategy.

A new company, New Zealand Steel Development (NZSD), was formed for the purpose, owned 60% by the government and 40% by New Zealand Steel. Stage 2 started at Glenbrook in 1982.

Because the various unions could not see long-term employment opportunities, demarcation disputes developed among them to prolong contracts. As the government was the major shareholder in NZSD the project was dogged by labour strikes, and the delays, together with high inflation rates, caused big cost overruns.

The development of the original works expansion continued with the commissioning of the pre-painting line in 1982. Total output at this time averaged 300,000 tonnes per annum.

Muldoon's snap election strategy failed him and in 1984 David Lange's new Labour government soon made it clear that they favoured neither state assistance to industry nor market protection. Accumulated losses, low world steel prices and higher coal prices meant that the new government had to come up with more money. They forced New Zealand Steel to renegotiate the arrangement it had made with the Muldoon government, agreeing in return to take over the NZSD loans. The company had to forfeit its coal and electricity price concessions, its market protection and the New Zealand Steel Development loan guarantees. New Zealand Steel was required to buy the government share in the development company and issue New Zealand Steel shares ~ effectively the government became the majority shareholder of New Zealand Steel.

Although selling galvanised coil and ironsand made some profit, the government had to keep coming up with more cash because of inflation and the mounting cost of the new development.

In 1986 an 18 km, 187mm diameter slurry pipeline was completed to bring ironsand direct to the mill from Waikato North Head ~ again, pioneering stuff. This was the world's first polyurethane-lined high-pressure underground pipeline for pumping abrasive granular materials, and it created a world slurry pumping record. It carries around 1.5 million tonnes per year.

The same year, after a capital reconstruction, the government acquired an 81% shareholding that increased the next year to 90%. In 1987 the expansion programme was completed and New Zealand Steel became a fully integrated steelworks, producing flat steel products solely from local sand.

The day before the 1987 sharemarket crash the government sold New Zealand Steel to Alan Hawkins' Equiticorp for $343 million, a sixth of its cost. To many this appeared to be a shady deal and it came as no surprise that the government was successfully sued for some of the loss due to the sale and that Alan Hawkins was later jailed for fraud. The Hawkins conglomerate owned the company for just over a year before a statutory receiver was appointed in 1989. In the same year the receiver accepted an ownership tender from Minmetals, a Chinese-based steel conglomerate, but this deal collapsed around the time of the Tiananmen Square debacle. This was just as well, as rumour had it that the total works would have been dismantled and rebuilt somewhere in the vast plains of China.

Hot-rolled material leaves the coil-box midpoint in the transformation from slab to coil.
New Zealand Steel

Finished coils awaiting dispatch from Glenbrook.
NZ STEEL DESIGN GUIDE 1986

Rolls of coil ~ ten tonnes worth.
NEW ZEALAND STEEL

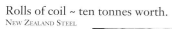

Although Fletcher Challenge was still interested in buying New Zealand Steel, the company was bought later that year by the Helenus Corporation, whose shareholders were Fisher & Paykel, Steel & Tube, ANZ Bank (NZ) Group and BHP (Pty) Co.

In 1992 BHP acquired an 81% interest by buying out Fisher & Paykel and Steel & Tube, and the company was renamed BHP New Zealand Steel.

In addition to producing hot-dipped galvanised sheet and coil, the existing continuous galvanising line was modified in 1994 to produce the aluminium/zinc alloy Zincalume.

In 2001 BHP merged with the huge British resources group Billiton, and BHP Steel was spun out as a separate Australian publicly listed company. In 2003 BHP New Zealand Steel was once again renamed New Zealand Steel.

New Zealand Steel was a political football during its formative years. The Labour government's free-market Rogernomics philosophy did not fit comfortably with a government-owned steel mill, and they wanted out.

There is a certain irony in the political u-turn whereby National under Muldoon sponsored New Zealand Steel as a state-owned and operated venture, and Labour sold it off with the rest of the family silver.

However, if government assistance had not been provided, we would not have a significant steel industry, and every year the current account deficit would be some $600 million higher.

New Zealand Steel remains the world's only producer of steel from ironsand, with total annual production of approximately 700,000 tonnes, and is this country's largest single-site employer. Although the company is no longer locally owned or controlled, full credit must be given to Sir Woolf Fisher, Sir John Ingram and all those who believed that we would make steel from ironsand. We have a great New Zealand success story here, but how many people realise today that their new corrugated iron roof originated from the ironsands on our beaches?

Typical New Zealand Steel annual production	
Input	Tonnes
Ironsand	1,200,000
Coal	700,000
Limestone	50,000
Output	
Hot rolled coil	700,000
Cold rolled coil	400,000
Metallic coated coil	200,000
Prepainted coil	50,000

This self-supporting roof cladding being placed at Takanini by Ebert Construction shows how far the concept of structural corrugate has come. The Z450 steel sheet uses the corrugating principle established by Richard Walker in 1821. The building is a grain store, and the lack of trusses and support columns means that dust and seeds can't accumulate, birds can't perch, and trucks can extend to 12 metres to tip their loads.
SIMON COTTER/PROGRESSIVE BUILDING MAGAZINE

New Zealand Steel, looking north. Hot and cold rolling mills on the left,
prepainting centre left, galvanising centre right, and the smelter by the river.

What's in a name?

The name *corrugated iron* has been technically incorrect for a century or more. Just as there is no egg in eggplant, no ham in hamburger and no duck in Bombay Duck, there is now no iron in corrugated iron ~ only steel.

There is little point in trying to change any of these names. If we are talking 19th century, corrugated iron is the correct term, but product made since then is likely to be steel.

The Latin *corrugare* is 'to make full of wrinkles' and the Italian word *galvanismo* is after Luigi Galvani, a physicist famous for generating electricity by chemical means and making frogs' legs twitch.

Most New Zealanders have some emotional attachment to corrugated iron but not everyone is in love with 'the corrugate'.

Corrugated iron was described in John Loudon's *Encyclopaedia of Cottage, Farm and Village Architecture* as "roofs that are composed of sheet iron impressed so as to present a surface of semicircular ridges with intervening furrows lengthwise of the sheet. Iron so furrowed will be preferable to common sheet iron coverings." In 1832 Loudon wrote, "Portable houses might be very readily made for exportation but wherever such houses were erected they should be covered with ivy or some evergreen creeper to moderate the effect of the change in exterior temperature."

It has been called names by prominent people, such as author Anthony Trollope:

> Corrugated iron does not make picturesque houses. Probably my readers all know the thin fluted material of which I speak, drawn out so fine that it can be cut like cloth with a pair of shears. It is very portable; easily shaped; capable of quick construction; and it keeps out the rain. It is, however, subject to drawbacks. The rooms of it of course are small, and every word uttered in the house can be heard throughout it, as throughout a shed put up without divisions.

John Ruskin predicted in 1848 that the time was probably near when a new system of architectural laws would be developed, adapted entirely to metallic construction.

An anonymous 19th century journalist, describing imported prefabricated buildings, says:

"Longest word I know's corrugated iron"

~ *Pallet on the Floor*, Ronald Hugh Morrieson,

Publisher Christine Roberts doing field research at Little River, on Banks Peninsula.

They are rapidly put together; but they should send out iron constitutions with them, for the people who are doomed to inhabit them; for they will be very cold in winter, and in summer will just roast their tenants alive. They will prove admirable houses ~ for the doctors.

Another 'nony mouse' English critic thought iron more suitable for poultry than people:

Corrugated iron shares the functional advantages and ugliness of its fibre equivalent, but can easily and effectively provide a roof on a poultry box or portable building. Its advantage is strength, and whereas it might dent it doesn't shatter like asbestos cement sheeting. Even when denied a periodic coating of paint, its life can exceed twenty-five years. Admittedly rust will eventually break through the zinc-coated surface ~ especially at coastal locations where salt-laden breezes hasten damage to ferrous metals. But whereas zinc-coated steel roofs last well, aesthetically they are not attractive. Furthermore, their performance in respect of thermal insulation ~ the ability to retain warmth in winter and to resist solar gain in summer ~ is negligible. As a roofing material, corrugated steel sheeting is better suited for the homes of poultry rather than people.

New Zealand playwright Bruce Mason asked cynically, "What kind of a society can develop under corrugated iron?" and poet Charles Brasch, in his *Indirections: A Memoir*, described "Raw shapeless towns, scattered thinly about the country like an unrelated, unassimilable scum of human tide-wrack, with their bleeding colour and unhuman corrugated iron."

Below: A work of art or a recycled hip roof? ~ north Wairarapa.
Terence Hodgson

Right: Patching with new iron is not a bright idea. Better to renew one half and patch with the old stuff.

COLIN MARTIN

Flo Fickle, who lived in Torbay
Changed her mind, like her smalls, every day
If you need any proof
Just look at her roof
Case rested ~ I've no more to say.

An extract from a London paper describes 'Hemming's houses':

> The first idea that strikes a stranger is that these buildings must be both insufferably hot and miserably cold. Now all this would most likely be the case with an iron house put up by a common builder but Mr Hemming is not simply a builder and a residence in tropical climates has taught him both what to provide for and what to provide against.
>
> A clear space of several inches betwixt the iron and the woodwork of the buildings and a wide space between the ceilings, of papered inodorous felt and the roof, secures an ample ventilation and equitable temperature.

Peter Tomory, director of the Auckland City Art Gallery, who in 1961 described New Zealand as a land inhabited by 60 million sheep and 2.5 million philistines, had a kinder view of corrugated iron: "There are many critics of weatherboard and corrugated iron but both materials have a curious felicity with the land and climate and it is interesting to compare both overlap and corrugation with the coruscated surfaces of Moorish architecture in Southern Spain, where there is the same brilliant light." (*Distance Looks Our Way*, 1961)

Hauraki farm shed.
JOCELYN CARLIN

Brands

Imported corrugated iron was paint-branded so that the mill which made it could be identified. Many of the ironworks were located in Wales because coal and iron were plentiful there.

Morewood & Rogers sold corrugated iron into New Zealand under the Dolphin brand until 1860. After this date the Gospel Oak Iron & Galvanised Iron and Wire Co exported Gospel Oak corrugated iron to New Zealand, until Baldwins acquired the brand in 1920 and used it until as late as 1939. Gospel Oak's brand had an anchor symbol between the G and O.

Lysaght's main brand was Orb and their cheaper version was marketed as Redcliffe. In 1920 rights to the Orb brand passed to John Lysaght Australia; their cheaper product was renamed Guinea. Lysaghts also sold some Globe. Crown brand was used for rainwater goods.

Corrugated iron brands identify the manufacturer, and sometimes when it was made, its thickness and coating weight.

A selection of
New Zealand brands,
old and new.

New Zealand Steel

From companies like Braby & Co we imported everything from galvanised iron wheelbarrows to corrugated iron sheds.

John Lysaght Australia's corrugated iron always included the words Lysaght Australia. The company introduced Red Orb in the early 1930s, using high-tensile steel intended for straight cladding and not suitable for curving. Since 1934 all Orb and Red Orb sheets have the date of manufacture printed as the last two digits of the year, placed within the Maltese cross at the top of the sphere. In 1950 Orb was changed to Blue Orb, which was used for curving verandahs and water tanks, and in 1967 Red Orb was replaced by Custom Orb.

The first New Zealand brand was Southern Cross, made by Samuel Parker in 1886. Ness Irwin's Longrun began in 1962 and was soon followed by Marshall's Pioneer brand. New Zealand Steel's brand of galvanised steel was called Galvsteel.

Manufacturers of imported corrugated iron

COMPANY	LOCATION	BRAND
F Braby & Co	Glasgow	Empress, Castle
Burnell & Co	England	Swallow
Davies Brothers & Co	Wolverhampton	Crown
Gospel Oak Works	Tipton, Staffordshire	Gospel Oak
John Lysaght (Australia)	Newcastle, Australia	Queens Head, Red Orb, Blue Orb, Custom Orb, (New) Guinea
John Lysaght (UK)	Bristol	Orb, Redcliffe, Globe, Crown
Morewood & Rogers	Llanelli, Wales	Dolphin
Raven Sheet & Galvanising Co	Glanamman, Wales	Raven
Richard Thomas Baldwin	Ebbw Vale	Spelterfast
Steel Company of Wales	Newport, Wales	SCW
John Summers	Shotton	Galvatite
Tupper & Co	Birmingham	Anchor, Pyramid
Others		Comet, Leopard, Lighthouse, Marksman, Phoenix, Titan, Windmill

Other overseas mills supplied steel for corrugate before New Zealand Steel began manufacturing its own. New Zealand Steel imported galvanised coil mostly from Japan, including River brand produced by the Kawasaki Mill. Some steel came from Yawata in Japan and Iscor in South Africa.

Wares made by the Southern Cross Galvanised Iron Manufacturing Company in Auckland. Apart from the sheets of corrugated iron at the back, there are galvanised water tanks, watering cans, buckets, baths, travelling trunks, coal scuttles, wood boxes, and boilers. The firm also produced enamelled products.
ALEXANDER TURNBULL LIBRARY PA1-0-371-38

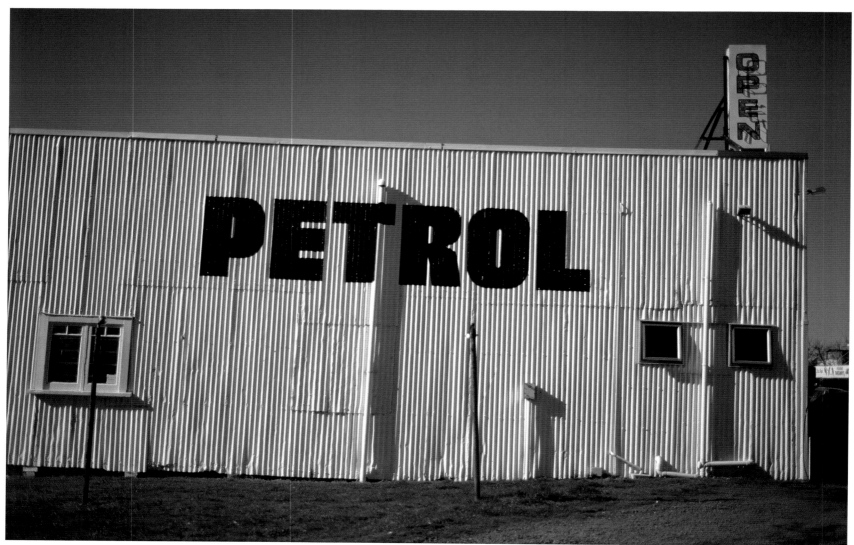

Shed in the Waikato.
Jocelyn Carlin

Today's fashion material

We now live in a throwaway society. Wearing out is not an option ~ we must stay in fashion and keep up with our peers. We shred clothes that are not worn out, crush cars that still go, throw away computers that still work and pull down houses and buildings because they are not 'economically viable'.

The temporary nature of New Zealand buildings is obvious after a visit overseas ~ the air of permanency about Europe's buildings is missing here. Our use of timber and corrugated iron reinforces that impression, but this downside of building in New Zealand (particularly residential) can also be regarded as an upside ~ we can change it instantly.

In the 21st century corrugated iron is trendy and has undergone an architectural rebirth. The haybarns that have dotted our rural landscape for decades have moved into the cities and suburbs. Multi-storey buildings are clad in it, we've lengthened it, strengthened it, turned it sideways and painted it rainbow colours. The pitched roof skyline to which we have become accustomed has now an increasing number of corrugated curves.

The building industry likes to keep up with fashion and architects and developers are constantly looking to attract new clients with the latest trends. Corrugated iron gives them the perfect opportunity.

Corrugated iron's face changes colour

Unlike Australia, where the naturally weathered look has been the most sought-after, we have always been keen to paint our roofs. When the Aussies did paint theirs they chose Battleship or Harbour Bridge Grey. Kiwis wanted their roofs to look distinctive, and because no part of New Zealand is more than 100km from the sea, regular painting has been needed to make corrugated iron last longer. Many early settlers and farmers used red lead or white lead mixed with linseed oil and terebene to make their own paint. Why buy it when you could make it? (As an apprentice I spent considerable time mixing up red lead in this manner to paint the laps of corrugated iron.)

Setting off the bush in Titirangi, Auckland.

I went to see my architect
Who was very highly rated
He really wants a smooth effect
But I want it corrugated.

Up to World War II the most popular roof colours here were Barn Red and Steelite Green. Years ago in Wellington a scandal broke out when a painter was seen in the wee hours of the morning repainting a large sign, with its original date still visible, which proclaimed 'watch this steelite green stay green'.

When acrylic paints first came on the market, paint companies advertised them as not requiring any primer, against the advice of the corrugate manufacturers. It didn't take long before these roofs were red with rust ~ almost as red as the paint manufacturers' faces.

Once continuous galvanising lines were established it was logical to paint metallic-coated coil before roll-forming it into roof cladding. Prepainted cladding has saved the house owner the cost of the three-yearly painting chore. Most broom-wielding amateurs (who produced a job to match) have welcomed the coming of pre-painted corrugate.

The first colour-coated steel coils for making corrugated iron in New Zealand were imported in the early 1960s from the newly nationalised mills of the British Steel Corporation.

British Steel originally produced two coatings, Organasol and Plastisol, and I imported these materials into the Thomson Metal Industries factory at Porirua. What a disaster! The trials of this material had been done in Europe where the UV radiation and climate is very different from ours. Because we had a guarantee the coatings were replaced without cost when they failed ~ but not the loss of reputation. Shortly after the material had been replaced it all happened again and two senior British Steel technical experts hotfooted it out to the 'colony' to see what was going on ~ despite our assurances that their coatings and not our method of production was at fault.

British Steel couldn't understand it. Only in Argentina and New Zealand had they seen delaminating faults like this ~ our UV simply destroyed the stuff. Material was then replaced without charge with the Rolls-Royce of newly developed laminates (not a paint) named Stelvetite, which was adhered to a galvanised coil and came with a 25-year guarantee.

What happened next was embarrassing to say the least. Within two years disaster struck again and this time I beat a hasty track to the UK to see what was going on. There were manufacturing faults and the material had just been stuck on without being pre-treated adequately or primed. Under our severe conditions, the film (dark colours particularly) simply came unstuck.

British Steel honoured their guarantee but must have lost a heap of money over the excursion into colour-coated steel for New Zealand roofs. Needless to say it was not a good start for us either. In the years between 1960 and 1982 paint technology made giant strides and we learnt a lot about New Zealand conditions.

Our first continuous paint-coating line was up and running in the 1960s in the Hunter Douglas factory at Auckland. They painted miles of narrow aluminium venetian blind material and in 1976 took a major leap of faith and commissioned a 1200mm-wide paint line.

Hunter Douglas painted customers' galvanised coils for corrugate up to 1981 and painted all of New Zealand Steel's coloured steel material from 1980 to 1982. In 1982 New Zealand Steel set up a colour-coating line at Glenbrook and launched its product as Colorsteel.

Hunter Douglas launched their own painted coil as ColorCote later in 1982, and the company was reformed to become Pacific Coilcoaters in 1988. It is a fully owned subsidiary of Fletcher Building Ltd.

Colour fading has been a problem over the years and both New Zealand Steel and Pacific Coilcoaters have made numerous changes to primers and topcoats. They both continue to upgrade their coating systems as paint technology improves.

To the layperson this has been confusing because the description of coatings keeps changing. They are (or have been) sold under different tradenames or descriptions, which include 5000, 8000, 8500, G2, FL, GR6, GR8, VP, G2Z, GRX, ZR8, ZRX, AR8, ARX, Endura and Maxx.

Now your corrugated roof can be any colour you wish and comes with a guarantee to match. It pays to remember that darker colours will absorb more heat and expand more. They are more likely to creak and bang when you least expect it!

Flashings

A flashing is a metal covering which prevents water from getting into the building. Word has it that some architects do not like flashings ~ in fact, a few would rather have no flashings at all. The minimalist look extends now to roof overhangs, where the bare bones of a building are naked and corrugate is blatantly exposed to view, and to the elements.

Townhouses in Auckland, seaside house in Wellington.

Flashings. Ridging for corrugated iron had a thin strip of lead soldered to its edge which could easily be hammered down to conform to the corrugations. Lead is no longer used for this purpose, as it is not compatible with Zincalume. I used to solder the eight-foot lead strips on contract after work, if I was not at night tech. My record was 36 strips in an hour.

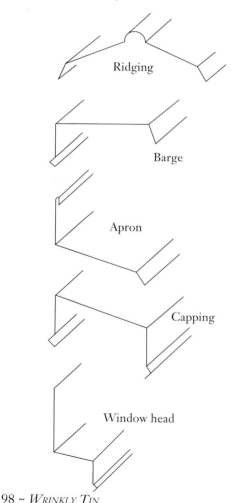

Ridging

Barge

Apron

Capping

Window head

Flashings serve a double purpose: they provide a weatherproof edge to roof cladding and give structural stability to the edges of the sheeting. The wind force around the outside edges of a roof can be twice that in the centre and demands double the number of fasteners. If you are thinking about leaving off barge flashings … *don't.*

Curving

Corrugate can be curved by machine or by naturally draping it.

Spring curving is the term used in roofing when continuous lengths of corrugate are draped naturally between eaves, with no ridging. It is also known as draping or arching and is suited to high-strength sheeting that can follow a curve without much distortion.

To roll-curve sheets to a smaller or specific radius, a machine is used ~ this is *pre-curving*. Pre-curved cladding is used where a radius is too small for draping curved roofs, such as those required for bullnosed verandahs or ridges.

Sheets are passed several times through a curving machine with pyramid rolls, which by adjustment progressively forms the curve to the correct radius. Low-strength steel must be used for machine-curving corrugated cladding, which can be curved down to a 300mm radius.

When John Lysaght first started making high-strength steel corrugated iron they printed a red warning on their Red Orb: 'Not for curving'.

The New Zealand Building Code minimum pitch requirement for corrugated iron is 8°. You don't have to be a rocket scientist to recognise that the roof pitch of a curved roof does not comply.

Question: How can the New Zealand Building Code and curved roofs be reconciled?

Answer: Where a curved roof is almost flat at the crest, the side laps are fastened and sealed to provide drainage over the top of the arch until the 8° minimum roof pitch is reached.

Laps

The *side lap* of corrugate is where a sheet overlaps another lengthwise down the roof to provide a weatherproof seal. The *end lap* is where sheets overlap one another, laterally (transversely) or across the roof. The rusting of end laps of galvanised corrugated iron used to be a problem, but now sheets can be cut to exact length without the need for end laps.

Before the advent of continuous manufacture of corrugate from coil, sheets were made eight corrugations wide with an 'over' on each side which had two nesting laps. Side laps often rusted out, but end laps were much worse, even with priming. Many people thought that corrosion occurred due to water's capillary action, but mostly it was due to condensation running down the inside of the sheets. Corrugate now has ten and a half corrugations and is designed for one and a half laps, with an 'under' and an 'over'. Nowadays we do not prime side laps, but the top and bottom of any end lap must be sealed to avoid corrosion, even when using pre-painted corrugate.

As an impatient apprentice who couldn't wait for the laps to dry before nailing corrugated iron on a roof, I was guilty of just getting on with the job. When some of these sheets were removed decades later the transverse laps were in perfect condition, unlike most other primed laps. The sheets were sealed together, stuck by thick red lead primer. *Eureka!*

Some say
Curvaceous
Vivacious
Audacious
Flirtatious

Some say
Good gracious!

Mini-iron

Miniature corrugated iron was imported from Australia even in the 19th century. It was made in New Zealand by Thomas Ballinger in Wellington in 1897 and known as 'fineline corrugated'. Dan Cosgrove in Timaru and NS Irwin in Auckland have also produced 'baby iron' for many years.

Both companies produced 'mini' on a barrel corrugator from low-strength steel to the imperial measurement of a one-inch pitch and one quarter of an inch height. It is now roll-formed in long lengths in high-strength steel.

Although variously called baby iron, ripple iron, mini-corrugate, sparrow iron and mini-iron, it's really the same product. It is not a self-supporting structural profile like its big brother but is used for internal linings where framing is at 600mm centres.

Baby iron is used as wall cladding, for soffits and as an internal decorative panelling. It has found recent popularity with landscape designers.

Instant windows ~ corrugated plastic

Corrugated has another younger brother in the form of plastic translucent sheeting, made originally from PVC, then fibreglass and the 'Johnny-come-lately' ~ polycarbonate. The pragmatism of corrugated metal roof and wall cladding logically led to corrugated plastic sheeting.

There are some problems. Don't risk stepping on it, and condensation is a pain. Obviously there is no building paper underlay, so you have to either put up with the drips or provide a second skin.

It expands more than steel, so you should pre-drill oversize holes in all plastic sheeting to avoid the creaking associated with it.

The simplest way to use corrugated plastic sheeting is to place just one sheet on top of the metal because then its strength is enhanced by the metal sheeting on both sides. For relatively unskilled people this is easier than installing a window.

Auckland apartments clad in mini-iron.

Corrugated iron has a young baby brother
Called baby iron or wriggly tin
You'd have thought by all its wrinkles
That he would be older than him.

This retreat in the Hawkes Bay, designed by architects Bevin + Slessor and clad in mini-corrugate, combines the familiar simplicity of the Kiwi bach with all the comforts expected by people seeking luxury lodgings: www.MillarRoad.co.nz.

NICK BEVIN

The owners of this house in Havelock North liked the spacious feeling of old barns and woolsheds and initially looked for one to renovate and live in. After an unsuccessful search they commissioned architects Bevin + Slessor to create this house for them.
NICK BEVIN

Left: This clifftop Hokitika home, by Chris Middleditch of Arcdesign, faces the West Coast's wind and rain. Challenges to sheet laps and flashings were addressed by South Island specialist Calder Stewart Roofing.
ROOFLINK MAGAZINE

Above: BHP Colorbond features on this voluptuous Australian creation.
BHP

It is crinkly and is made by the tons
It comes in short and long runs
But when concave and convexy
The curves are quite sexy …
And remind me of Dolly Parton's ones

Materials for this Kapiti Coast bach, designed by Bevin + Slessor architects, had to be robust to withstand all the westerlies and intense UV light nature throws at the site.
Nick Bevin

This lakeside Rotorua home, pictured front and back, features Titania Colorsteel roofing.
NEW ZEALAND STEEL/GEOFF KIRKHAM

Some people say
It's a passing fashion
But architects love it
With a passion

Above: The design of Queenstown luxury lodge Muna Moke (www.munamoke.co.nz) was inspired by the *Earnslaw* steamer that plied Lake Wakatipu. Architect: Ed Elliott; builders: Peter and Paul Rogers of RBJ Ltd, Queenstown.
BRUCE JACKSON/COLORCOTE

Left: This house at Taylor's Mistake, Christchurch, is another featuring a curved corrugated roof which responds to its setting.
NEW ZEALAND STEEL/GEOFF KIRKHAM

The industrial look: Above, WestpacTrust Stadium, Wellington's 34,500-seat 'Cake Tin' may look like corrugate but is clad with a trapezoidal Dimond Roofing profile; the squared-off corrugations are a stronger version of corrugated iron. Architects: Warren & Mahoney.

Left and below left: This Wairarapa retreat designed by Nick Bevin has sliding corrugated walls which close fully for security … and open right out so that the wide open spaces can be enjoyed.

Below: *Trompe l'oeil* in Wellington ~ film-makers Gibson Group used corrugate to transform their bland concrete offices into a Kiwi shed.

New profile
Newly made
Is known as
Trapezoidal

Old profile
Always made
Is known as
Sinusoidal.

Keep it on: lead-heads & twisted shanks

In the 19th century the galvanised nail used to fix roof sheets had a heavy dome head with a forged chisel point and a lead washer. This was most likely the forerunner of the lead-head nail. Some early nails had a square shank with a diamond washer. Later, springhead nails were imported from Australia. They had a washer underneath the head welded together by the galvanising process. These were the farmers' favourite because they were cheap ~ what's a leak or two in a farm shed anyway!

A similar springhead nail was made by Samuel Parker in Auckland, called the Acme.

Lead-head nails were made in Wellington from 1864 onwards by Davenport & Son, said to be "supplying all parts of the colony in large quantities and for which they have made their name famous." In 1893 another Wellington company, Thomas Ballinger & Co, started making lead-heads, and they were the common nail for corrugated iron from the late 19th century until the 1970s.

From the 1940s onwards the best lead-heads came from a Christchurch company, AC Venables. I remember lifting many a full hundredweight (cwt) box of these nails. At 50kg that was twice the weight of the half-boxes sold today. Venables dipped rose-head nails into a bath of lead before upending them into a mould to cast a 'policeman's helmet' onto them. This nail was called the Alpha and had five advantages over the others:

• The shank was covered in lead which gave it good holding in wood
• The coating provided barrier protection and the nail did not rust
• The head was firmly stuck on, lead-to-lead
• The tapered thin lead skirt made a soft seal which followed the shape of the corrugation.
• The rose-head did not come off when the nail was struck.

An unfortunate fate befell this nail. Venables' manufacturing plant was bought by their opposition, the Auto Manufacturing Co, who not long after closed the factory down "for economic reasons". The only lead-head left on the market was an uncoated flat-head steel nail that fell apart when struck. A lead-head without a head.

HPF Weatherseal nails.
HYLTON PARKER FASTENERS

One of the main answers to cyclone damage: the load-spreading washers shown here under test keep the roof on.

Everyone knows	Gutter blocked-up
Story goes	Plumber rung-up
Wind blows	Delay hiccup
Storm grows	Wife hung-up
Rainwater flows	Man fix-up
Water hose	Insurance mix-up
Leak shows	Bill stick-up
Dilemma grows	Prize cock-up
Wet clothes	Everyone knows
Fingers froze	Story goes …

We used to fix our roofs on
With nails that had heads full of lead
The heads though never stayed on
So we now use screws instead.

The evolution of corrugated iron fasteners. From left: Hand-forged chisel-point nail with lead washer circa 1840, used on the Camphouse and Matanaka; spring head, the farmers' friend; lead-head ~ a little more sophistication; spiral shank ~ ever tried pulling one out; self-drilling Type 17 screw ~ quick and busy.

I once condemned this nail at a public forum and was threatened with legal action. The demise of the lead-head was assured because without a 'skirt' seal, the leaky nail quickly rusted away.

Lead-heads had a smooth shank and were prone to 'backing out'. This fault was so common that most agile homeowners had to hammer home loose lead-heads before each winter. Often they only succeeded in denting the iron and making matters worse. Some unscrupulous plumbers or roofers would find the leaks from the attic and put paint tins under them to avoid climbing up onto the roof. This 'repair' worked for a year or two before the tin rusted out. When the owner reported that the leak had come back in the same place fixed previously, the plumber would replace the paint tin!

Lead-heads, like lead-edged ridging, seem to be a homegrown New Zealand item; Australia has never taken to them.

Although twisted shank nails were available, it was not until the late 1970s that the long reign of the lead-head was over. Production of spiral shank nails by PKR (Pearson, Knowles & Reynolds) and then the Nu-way nail by Dimond Industries took over. The Nu-way nail was originally imported from South Africa and used a galvanising method known as *peen plating*. It was later made at Dimond's Seaview factory in Wellington. Production was then taken over by PKR.

Annular groove nails were also made but were not popular, because holding the rough-shaped and galvanised nail while hammering it in tended to remove the skin from the thumb and forefinger. Sore fingers also happened to a lesser degree with spiral shank nails.

After 1980 Hylton Parker Fasteners began making Weatherseal spiral shank nails in Auckland, initially only zinc-plated. Shortly afterwards the coating was changed to hot-dipped zinc and made with a softer seal than the Nu-way nail. To match the ever-increasing use of colour-coated corrugated iron, suppliers and roofers began to paint their own nails, often with dire results. In 1983 Hylton Parker introduced colour caps (which had a bad habit of popping off) and later began manufacturing colour-painted nails.

Problems with spiral shank nails backing out still occur occasionally because of the fluctuating moisture content and the lower density of pinus radiata purlins compared to rimu.

Self-drilling screws have always been an option for fixing corrugated iron, but because they were twice the price of nails they were used less here than they were in Australia.

Portable screw guns have made screws more popular because they are quick, and easy on the fingers. The screw is an overkill for withdrawal strength, but because it has a smaller head than the nail washer, sheets are more prone to 'blow over the top' ~ leaving the screw still in the timber but the metal cracked around the hole.

Screws are easy to use because they drill their own hole in the corrugated iron and stop automatically, if the screw gun is properly set. They used to be hot-dipped galvanised but now are mostly peen-plated to provide corrosion resistance equal to that of the corrugated iron.

Screws and nails must have a sealing washer under their head, and in areas around the outside of the roof, larger shaped load-spreading washers should be used ~ particularly in Wellington!

Make your roof stay on and last longer

- If your curved roof is a porch or has exposed eaves without any lining, the underside of the sheeting is protected from the weather. The rain won't wash it, so you have to ~ regularly.
- When such a building is close to the sea the soffit (eaves) should be lined.
- If you want to walk on your roof, keep close to the purlin and spread your feet over several corrugations, walking crabwise up the roof.
- If you weigh more than 100kg, stay off. Get somebody else to clean the gutters.
- Space purlins around the outside of your roof closer than the middle ones.
- Verandah roofs and plastic sheets should also have purlins spaced closer than normal.
- If you live in an exposed area, use extra fixings and load-spreading washers. You'll need them for the big one!
- Where curved sheets need to be joined, condensation can run down the inside of the cladding and into the end laps, causing corrosion. The paint coating won't stop it, so seal all end laps.
- Do not flatten roofing sheets when hammering nails or driving screws.
- Do not re-use corrugated roof cladding when the profile has been damaged.
- To reduce the chance of your roof blowing off, ventilate the attic.
- Always use barge flashings.
- If you are into serious DIY, buy the *Metal Roof and Wall Cladding Code of Practice* from www.metalroofing.org.nz

Cyclone wailing
Building failing
Iron sailing
Not enuf nailing

A man needs a home to call his
To shelter his family in
A home's a home wherever it is
Even when made out of tin

It's not bought, just gathered up after the last storm.

The sad reality is that tyres, timber
and rocks will not save this roof
when the next cyclone strikes.

Corrugating the Pacific ...

Before the 1980s New Zealand used to export corrugated iron to the Pacific, but subsequently a number of redundant machines in New Zealand found their way offshore, enabling locals to make it themselves in the most unlikely places. Lysaghts started manufacturing in Fiji and Reddy-Dimond followed soon after in Lautoka and Suva. New Zealand has always taken an interest in the islands; besides being a place to sell coil, they have become a testing ground for performance under extreme conditions. Making roofs hold on during cyclones has become a sharp learning curve for all involved.

The expediency of the material was not lost on Pacific Islanders who had few possessions of their own. After cyclones, corrugated iron could be salvaged, claimed and recycled. Without building controls, the piles of corrugated iron became squatters' settlements overnight. These shanties are the first to blow away again in the next storm and turn into flying debris that can be lethal.

The Rotary Club started a programme in Fiji in 1985 to house people who had no job, no money, and little chance of betterment without external help. Help came in the name of Levin-born Rotarian Peter Drysdale, who has spent most of his life in Fiji. With the help of Rotarians worldwide Peter built 700 Rotahomes ~ modest 12m² corrugated iron huts that were a safe improvement on makeshift shanties. Although these homes have been criticised as hotboxes, they have shutter windows on all sides and are a pragmatic, achievable solution.

Considerable damage has been caused in the Pacific Islands by corrugated iron blowing off roofs. Severe cyclone damage to buildings occurs with such regularity that there are obvious problems to address ~ firstly that some methods used to repair buildings are inadequate.

New materials are hard to come by and some people can't afford them anyway. Resources and training are needed to help Pacific Islanders fix the problems. All too often the owner flattens out the damaged iron and simply nails it back on with straightened nails, and not spiral shank ones either. Another reason that corrugated iron blows off is because flashings are considered an avoidable cost.

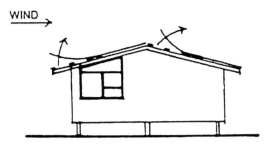

Failure: Wind lifts roofing off purlins
Remedy: More fasteners through roofing material

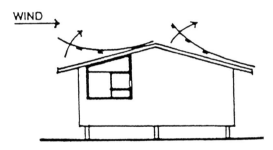

Failure: Wind lifts roofing and purlins together
Remedy: Adequate fixing of purlins to rafters

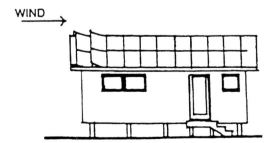

Failure: Wind lifts roofing off purlins
Remedy: More fasteners through roofing material and a suitable fascia barge flashing adequately fixed. Do not use a rolled edge flashing.

A cyclone warning brings memories of past trauma
It unleashes a fear of the unknown
The question of one's very survival
The howl rising to a screech
When everything is dark because the lights are gone
Calling the family and their precious warmth huddled together
The tearing wrench as the roof leaves the blackened sky to view
And the needles of rain which seem to last forever
Then the silence of the eye, an unreal heavy presence
A brief moment to view the destruction
To see the iron wrapped around the trees
Before the dreaded return from a changed direction
What chance our puny efforts
To stop nature's rampage?

Supported by Rotary clubs worldwide,
over 700 Rotahomes have been built in Fiji.

This practical DIY book was written by Stuart Thomson, printed by Rotary and distributed free to the Pacific Islands as a service project.

The way that a roof fails in a cyclone is commonly misunderstood. Failure usually starts at the roof overhang, balcony or gable end, followed by a catastrophic domino effect. The roof may appear to explode, but failure often starts because of one nail.

People become complacent and some rely on a few concrete blocks to hold their roof on. With recent cyclones occurring at night (with fewer people out and about) and better warning systems, there has been little loss of life. Schools roofs with wide verandahs are vulnerable but fortunately cyclones mostly come during the Christmas school holidays.

... and the Himalayas

When Sir Edmund Hillary began his expeditions to Nepal to assist the Sherpa people, it was not surprising that the schools and hospitals his teams built were roofed with corrugate. Although still the familiar corrugate profile, most of the material was not steel but aluminium, which had a distinct weight advantage over steel. I know this from personal experience because I was privileged to be part of those expeditions, and throwing sheets around at 12,000 feet is not like it is at home. Thirty years on, the roof cladding is doing fine.

The curvability of corrugate lends itself well to *fale* roofing in Samoa, as on these parliamentary buildings near Apia.

How does this sherpa negotiate this track when it narrows? ... very carefully.

"A sheet of iron became a cloth of light."

Left: A 1960s work by Blenheim's John Parker, who was among New Zealand's earliest corrugated iron artists. Having begun to work with iron while studying under Rudolf Gopas at Ilam School of Fine Arts in 1966, Parker was influenced by the cultural movement that rejected middle-classness. He liked the idea of using an affordable (or free) colonial material in a series of works that were essentially anti-art. "By crumpling and putting rents in roofing iron I changed a stiff and obstinate material into something more plastic. A sheet of iron became a cloth of light." Parker had first been attracted to the material while working among sheds and haybarns on Canterbury farms. Since his work, hundreds of New Zealand artists have experimented with the material.

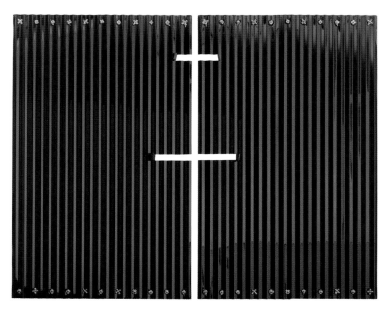

Right: Ralph Hotere's *Round Midnight*.

Far right: Ralph Hotere's *Aramoana*.

Iron in the spirit ~ corrugated art

We have many talented sculptors and artists but few have seen the potential of corrugated iron like New Zealand's 'Mr Corrugate' ~ Jeff Thomson.

Jeff left Elam School of Fine Arts in Auckland in 1989 and took time out travelling around New Zealand. He saw first-hand the influence of the ubiquitous corrugated iron on our rural and suburban scenes. Jeff says it all started while on a trek from Bulls to New Plymouth:

> I picked up a sheet of rusty red corrugated roofing iron and made a small cow out of it, which sat on top of a mailbox. Someone found out who made it and commissioned a tiger, a penguin and an elephant out of corrugated iron. Someone else who saw the elephant commissioned a fence of elephants because they'd had a dispute about their boundary fence and commissioned the elephants to sit with their backsides facing their neighbours. Over the next few years I got many commissions for tin animals for people's homes, and it developed into a full-time business.

Wild iron

Sea go dark, dark with wind,
Feet go heavy, heavy with sand,
Thoughts go wild, wild with the sound
Of iron on the old shed swinging, clanging:
Go dark, go heavy, go wild, go round,
Dark with the wind,
Heavy with the sand,
Wild with the iron that tears at the nail
And the foundering shriek of the gale.

~ Allen Curnow

Jeff Thomson's wandering herd in Albert Park, Auckland, and their corrugated calling card.
John Miller

Jeff Thomson.

Who is the man all tattered and torn
That made the cow with the crumpled horn,
That made the chook that crowed in the morn,
That made the Holden that looks forlorn?
~ Jeff Thomson.

Although the 'art hierarchy' may not entirely approve, average Kiwis empathise with Jeff's work simply because they understand it. He has taken what is essentially a two-dimensional form and added a third dimension, and in doing so has become almost as much a national identity as the material itself. An unpredictable one, as Jeff explained to me:

> In a sense I do have a signature in that I work with roofing materials such as corrugated iron to make a variety of objects, but my approach always has been and still is experimental. I really have no idea what I will be making in a month's time.
>
> In my studio I have a library of hundreds of old coloured corrugated iron sheets. In 1991 I corrugated my car and drove it for three years in New Zealand and in Australia. I received sponsorship from BHP, which covered the cost of the freight across the Tasman.

Jeff is a sculptor, a roofer, a wrecker, a builder and a 'tin basher'. He also happens to be one of the few who can make a living out of his art. He must have felt at home in Australia because they are the other country which has taken to corrugated iron ~ not so much for city roofs, where tiles are commonplace, but in rural Australia where the water tank and the bullnosed verandah hold sway.

Jeff reminisces: "Sleeping out in my corrugated Holden was like listening to the rain on the roof at home." His work is 'full-in-your-face' stuff, immediately recognisable by fans and strangers alike. This is not esoteric art, but is earthy, populist and very New Zealand. Jeff is an international artist and regularly exhibits in Germany, the United States and Australia.

The famous gumboot on State Highway 1 happened because Taihape, along with other rural communities, was facing problems. In the 1980s it was badly affected by the downsizing of New Zealand Railways and by the removal of government subsidies for fertiliser and other items. The population of the town fell from 3500 in the early '60s to 1500 in 1985. To survive, the town needed to take action. Late in 1984 Taihape decided to base its promotion on comedian John Clark's alter ego Fred Dagg and his gumboots, and the first Gumboot Day was held in 1985 with gumboot throwing, gumboot races, and other rural attractions.

> "Clouds with grey torn bellies came at eye level from the sea, dropping rain as fat as bantam eggs. It thickened up and thundered on my roof. When I put the new living-room on I made the roof iron (wriggly tin) so I could bring storms inside my house. It's like living at the back of a waterfall sometimes."
> ~ Maurice Gee, *Prowlers*

Jeff Thomson was asked to make a suitable sculpture for Taihape as the Gumboot Capital of the World, and now it is there for all to see.

In 2000 Jeff took up an opportunity to set himself up as a roofer when he was artist-in-residence at Wanganui's Tylee Cottage. He screen-printed corrugated iron ridgings and downpipes with his own brand of coloured steel art. Jeff has come full circle; he has made the whole house a work of art, a colourful, whimsical shelter reminiscent of the settler's cottage, complete with water tank. This is the house that Jeff built.

Who else has a corrugated roof with Jeff Thomson's screen printing on it?

A middle-earth New Zealand town
You used to drive right through
Had the Taihape Council worried
They didn't know what to do

They thought up lots of crazy things
To stop tourists on their route
But by far the best of them
Was throwing an old gumboot.

They now have a fun competition
Which depends on sex and size
But the one who throws the furthest
Is the one that takes the prize

To bring the town to your notice
They've an image that's a hoot
Jeff Thomson's ginormous sculpture
Of a krinkly tin gumboot.

This convoluted elephant
Is made of wrinkly tin
He lives alone at Auckland Zoo
Just right where you come in

This elephant is an African
You can tell it by the ears
He's loved by children everywhere
And some of older years

This huge and krinkly elephant
Is a one-off breed
Cos he is the only one
You'll never have to feed

JEFF THOMSON

Jeff Thomson's old tin Holden
That raced down at Te Rapa
Is now grow'n quite olden
And is parked up at Te Papa

Many artists (Grahame Sydney is perhaps best-known) have used corrugate to capture nostalgia for life beyond the city. These paintings from one Wellington gallery are but a small sample.
Above: 'Salt River Store' by Philip Kilmore
Above right: 'Corrugated iron and No 8 wire' by Brian McCracken
COURTESY THE ARTISTS & FISHER FINE ARTS, WELLINGTON

Opposite: 'Tower of Words/Tower of Silence'. This tower on Waiheke Island was conceived by sculptor Virginia King and designed in collaboration with her architect husband Mike.
VIRGINIA KING

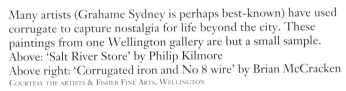

Rain on the roof

My nephew sleeping in a basement room
has put a sheet of iron outside his window
to recapture the sound of rain falling on the roof.

I do not say to him, The heart has its own comfort for grief.
A sheet of iron repairs roofs only. As yet unhurt by the demand
that change and difference never show, he is still able
to mend damages by creating the loved rain-sound
he thinks he knew in early childhood.

Nor do I say, In the travelling life of loss
iron is a burden, that one day he must find
within himself in total darkness and silence
the iron that will hold not only the lost sound of the rain
but the sun, the voices of the dead, and all else that has gone.

~ Janet Frame

Two houses by Jeff Thomson, installed at sculpture exhibitions. Above, on the North Shore; right, the 'coloured steel' house beside the Michael Fowler Centre, Wellington.
COLIN MARTIN

Below: 'Sylvia's Simca' (detail) by Philip Kilmore
COURTESY THE ARTIST & FISHER FINE ARTS, WELLINGTON

This house is made of corrugated tin
It's the smallest one you've ever bin in
All coloured up like a patchwork quilt
It is a house Jeff Thomson built.

JOCELYN CARLIN

Tirau's shepherd watches cars all day
All driving through the town
If he could talk I think he'd say
Keep your #*2%$#@& speeding down!

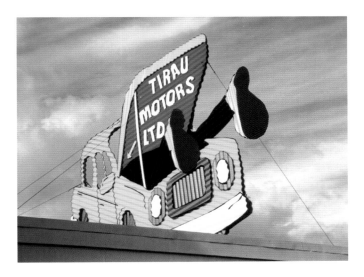

Jean Cash

Because it's on the main road through the centre of the North Island at just the right distance for a comfort stop, there would be few Kiwis who have not seen Tirau's claim to fame.

Some towns like Taihape and Otorohanga
Have pinched Tirau's arty phenomena
Who next it will be
We'll just have to see
Will it be Tauranga or Whangamomona?

The town of Tirau
Is the spot to see now
It owes its culture
To corrugated sculpture.

Yes, it's corrugated iron ~ made by Jeff
Thomson for the Wearable Arts competition.
Left: 'Flora', 2004; Right: 'Untitled', 2003.

Again, tonight I hear you rain,
    ironing out the corrugations on
    my tin roof, my worried brow …

~ *Hone Tuwhare*

Where to from here?

It arrived in the 1840s, boomed in the 19th century, grew in the 20th and is still making an impression in the 21st. This 'temporary' material seems to have been here forever and shows no signs of relinquishing its leadership in the cladding business. Its dominance has been challenged by a range of more sophisticated materials but corrugated iron is still No 1 and quintessentially New Zealand. Along with No 8 fencing wire, it can take the credit for fostering the Kiwi's love of 'giving it a go' and enabling would-be builders of anything to have a shot.

The times they are a-changing. The Building Act 2004 requires that all restricted building work must be carried out by a licensed building practitioner, and this effectively closes the era of DIY corrugate. From 2009 you will no longer be allowed to nail corrugated iron onto your own house. You will be able to fix it on to your henhouse (if you have the Ministry's permission) or a farm shed or a fence but sorry, not on your bach any more.

A problem, however, is only a solution in disguise. The same entrepreneurial spirit that imbued our early settlers ~ their pragmatism, compromise and stubbornness ~ will ensure that bureaucratic regulations do not prevent corrugated iron from retaining its rightful place in NZ.

New Zealand without corrugated iron … it's unthinkable.

To use corrugate you need an LBP[1]
To be PC you need a PC[2]
Some regs are OK
But you got to pay
But they would know best ~ yeah, right.

1. Licensed Building Practitioner
2. Product Certificate

There seems to be a parallel that can be drawn between
A common friend, a convoluted metal, that ubiquitous icon
That offers shelter on the way, that comforts many,
That protects from harm, that raises a smile,
All with a quiet humility
That shares our inevitability
To return whence it came.

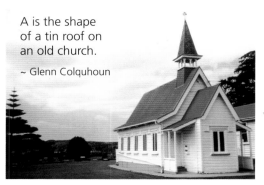

A is the shape
of a tin roof on
an old church.

~ Glenn Colquhoun

St Paul's Anglican church in Chapel Road,
East Tamaki was built in 1886 and is still in use.

Clock, publisher's office;
bench, Te Papa.

Reroofing St Peters church in Wellington. The roofer doesn't have a harness because edge protection is in place.
STEPHEN A'COURT PHOTOGRAPHY

Stuart Thomson and the *Code of Practice* he wrote for New Zealand metal roof and wall cladding.

Some say I'm a bit of a goof
And if you want the real proof
My pleasure in bed
Is the sound in my head
Of rain on my wrinkly tin roof

About the author

Stuart Thomson has been associated with corrugated iron most of his life. As a young boy he helped his plumber father and later became an apprentice plumber and sheet metal worker. Making tanks, repairing old roofs and installing new ones were all part of the trade at that time. After his apprenticeship Stuart worked his way to the UK on a ship and found work as a plumber and roofer in London.

Having observed first-hand methods of manufacture at steel and aluminium mills in Europe, he returned to New Zealand and set up Thomson Metal Industries in Wellington. In 1963 he built this country's first roll-former for secret-fix roof cladding, and other roll-formers to make roof claddings and accessories.

In 1973 and 1975 Stuart was invited by Sir Edmund Hillary to join his building programme in Nepal. He made and installed solar water heaters at Kunde and Saleri hospital and put corrugated roofs on a number of schools in the mountains.

Thomson Metal Industries was sold to Dimond Industries in 1977 and Stuart became their technical manager. In 1982 he went to New Zealand Steel as development engineer and designed the Steelspan roofing profile for its Glenbrook mill. Stuart wrote the first Profile Metal Cladding handbook and in 1984 he investigated cyclone damage in Fiji and consequently designed load-spreading washers for corrugated iron.

In 1988 he retired from New Zealand Steel and in 1993 designed and supervised the building of sixteen Cyclone Rotashelters (with corrugated roofs) for Samoa. His interest in the Pacific continued in 1995 when he designed and built a community hall at Ba, Fiji and in 1997 he returned to design and build fourteen earth-brick Rotacottages.

Stuart was granted honorary membership of the New Zealand Metal Roofing Manufacturers Inc in 1998 and in 2000 was commissioned to write their *New Zealand Metal Roof and Wall Cladding Code of Practice*, published in 2003. He is currently a member of several joint New Zealand/Australian Standards committees and practising as a building consultant.